The Judas Effect

The Judas Effect
How Evangelicals Betrayed Jesus for Power

Amy Hawk

CASCADE *Books* • Eugene, Oregon

THE JUDAS EFFECT
How Evangelicals Betrayed Jesus for Power

Copyright © 2024 Amy Hawk. All rights reserved. Except for brief quotations in critical publications or reviews, no part of this book may be reproduced in any manner without prior written permission from the publisher. Write: Permissions, Wipf and Stock Publishers, 199 W. 8th Ave., Suite 3, Eugene, OR 97401.

Cascade Books
An Imprint of Wipf and Stock Publishers
199 W. 8th Ave., Suite 3
Eugene, OR 97401

www.wipfandstock.com

PAPERBACK ISBN: 978-1-6667-6364-5
HARDCOVER ISBN: 978-1-6667-6365-2
EBOOK ISBN: 978-1-6667-6366-9

Cataloguing-in-Publication data:

Names: Hawk, Amy, author.

Title: The Judas effect : how evangelicals betrayed Jesus for power / by Amy Hawk.

Description: Eugene, OR : Cascade Books, 2024 | Includes bibliographical references and index.

Identifiers: ISBN 978-1-6667-6364-5 (paperback) | ISBN 978-1-6667-6365-2 (hardcover) | ISBN 978-1-6667-6366-9 (ebook)

Subjects: LCSH: Church and social problems—Evangelicalism. | Religion and sociology—Evangelicalism | Evangelicalism—United States—History—21st century.

Classification: BR1642.U5 H40 2024 (paperback) | BR1642.U5 H40 (ebook)

VERSION NUMBER 06/19/24

Unless otherwise indicated, all Scripture quotations are taken from The Message, copyright © 2018 by Eugene H. Peterson. Used by permission of NavPress. All rights reserved. Represented by Tyndale House Publishers, a Division of Tyndale House Ministries.

Scriptures marked NIV are taken from the NEW INTERNATIONAL VERSION (NIV): Scripture taken from THE HOLY BIBLE, NEW INTERNATIONAL VERSION®. Copyright © 2011 by Biblica, Inc.™ Used by permission of Zondervan.

Scripture quoted by permission. Quotations designated (NET) are from the NET Bible® copyright © 2019 by Biblical Studies Press, L.L.C. http://netbible.com. All rights reserved.

Scripture quotations marked (NASB®) taken from the New American Standard Bible®, copyright © 1995 by The Lockman Foundation. Used by permission. All rights reserved.

Scripture marked (NCV) taken from the New Century Version®. Copyright © 2005 by Thomas Nelson. Used by permission. All rights reserved.

Scripture quotations marked (RSV) taken from the Revised Standard Version of the Bible, copyright © 1971 National Council of the Churches of Christ in the United States of America. Used by permission. All rights reserved worldwide.

Scripture quotations marked (ESV) are from the ESV® Bible (The Holy Bible, English Standard Version®), copyright © 2001 by Crossway, a publishing ministry of Good News Publishers. Used by permission. All rights reserved.

AUTHOR'S NOTE

Dear Reader,

I write of Judas Iscariot as a disciple of Christ who disregarded the teachings of, and ultimately betrayed, his Teacher.

Sadly, I've since discovered that there is a long history of Christian anti-Semitism that uses Judas's betrayal as a basis for its hateful ideology.

Please note that it is my express wish that nothing I've written would cause harm or offense to the Jewish community. In no way should this book be used to further the tradition of Christian anti-Semitism.

Amy

For the church, whom Jesus dearly loves

My dear, dear friends! I love you so much. I do want the very best for you. You make me feel such joy, fill me with such pride. Don't waver. Stay on track, steady in God.

—Phil 4:1

Be wary of false preachers who smile a lot, dripping with practiced sincerity. Chances are they are out to rip you off some way or other. Don't be impressed with charisma; look for character. Who preachers *are* is the main thing, not what they say. A genuine leader will never exploit your emotions or your pocketbook.

—Matt 7:15–19

Contents

Preface—The Judas Effect | xi
Introduction | xv

1 Fly High with Hawk | 1
2 Trump Happens | 7
3 False Messiah | 12
4 Never Bow to a Bully | 20
5 Everything Is Uncovered | 28
6 The Fox | 35
7 Spritzing for Jesus | 40
8 An Open Door for the Devil | 43
9 Test the Spirits | 49
10 Grabbing Anything | 75
11 The Contaminated Gospel | 80
12 Human Scum | 87
13 The Power of Life and Death | 91
14 Welcome to Adventureland | 99
15 Choose Life | 103
16 Leave Her Alone | 106
17 Lusting for Power | 113

18 Wisdom from Hell | 119
19 Deborah's Daughters | 125
20 Lead Us Not | 129
21 Be Zealous and Repent | 136

Epilogue | 141
Recommended Reading | 143
Acknowledgments | 145
Subject Index | 147
Scripture Index | 151

Preface

The Judas Effect

Judas Iscariot was a follower of Jesus. He walked with him. He talked with him. He ate with him. Presumably, he participated with him in sharing the good news. He did everything a good follower of Jesus is supposed to do. But somewhere along the way his heart was tempted to go off mission. He became greedy for gain. It doesn't matter whether he wanted money or political power. Neither is promised to the follower of Christ.

Prior to his betrayal, Judas is revealed in Scripture to be something of a bully. When a woman interrupted his dinner to lavish Jesus with affection, Judas tried to intimidate her.[1] His displeasure at her showy demonstration of love gives us a glimpse into the inner workings of his heart. He prioritized power and money (and possibly image) over love. Thankfully, Jesus was quick to rebuke him.[2] It could be that Jesus's rebuke really angered Judas, because the next thing you know, "Judas began looking for an opportunity to betray him."[3]

We know how Judas's physical story ends—with his intestines spilled out in a field of blood. But the spirit that drove him toward betrayal didn't die. It's an attitude that will resort to bullying in order to get its own way. It's an attitude of greed, control, and intimidation tactics. It pretends to follow

1. John 12:4.
2. John 12:7.
3. Mark 14:10.

God even as it repels the people God is so desperately wanting to reach. It's an attitude alive and well in the church today.

The spirit of Judas will partner with anyone who prioritizes control and power over love. Besides greed, some signs of its presence are misogyny, a willingness to go along with lies, and a willingness to commit acts of violence. Where these attributes are present, you can be sure there has been a betrayal of Christ.

We have a tendency in evangelical spaces to point our fingers at those outside the church and accuse them of betraying Christ with blatant immorality. But "the world" cannot betray Christ; they haven't even met him. The one who has met him, walked with him, listened to him teach, followed and served him, and yet still calculates worldly power as more important than love of neighbor, character, or truth? He or she is the one who has committed betrayal.

* * *

In 2016, much of the (mostly white) American evangelical community allied with a man who bragged about grabbing women's genitals, called his opponents "stupid" and "pathetic," warned that Muslims and immigrants would take over our nation, boasted that he could shoot somebody on Fifth Avenue and wouldn't lose any voters, and declared himself to be "the only one" who could save us. Donald Trump threw out a net called "political power," and many white evangelicals jumped right into it. They did this to bring our nation closer to God.

As of this writing, our twice-impeached former president has been convicted on thirty-four counts of business fraud stemming from an illegal scheme to cover up sex scandals in advance of the 2016 election. The Trump Organization has been convicted of felony tax fraud and fined $1.6 million for evading taxes. In May 2023, a jury found Donald Trump liable in a civil case for $5 million for sexual abuse and defamation of E. Jean Carroll, one of the twenty-six women who have accused him of rape or sexual assault. In June, he was arraigned in federal court on thirty-seven criminal charges over his potential mishandling of classified White House documents, including willful retention of information pertaining to our national security. In early 2024, he was ordered to pay over $355 million for fraudulent business practices in New York. I have no idea what lies ahead for Trump, but I do know that many Evangelicals continue to offer their undying loyalty and support to him and send him money, despite his thieving and criminality. They have been led astray from their sincere and pure devotion to Christ.[4]

If the goal of Evangelicalism is to *repel* a harvest for Christ, partnering with Donald Trump was the right thing to do. But Christians are not here to amass power for ourselves. We are here to show people what Jesus looks like. We are here to show them the self-sacrificial, humble, truth-bearing, compassionate, others-oriented witness of Christ. This is so that, through our love and service, humanity may be reconciled to God. But instead, some Evangelicals set about effectively building up a wall of hostility that Christ already tore down. They followed Trump's lead instead of Christ's and showed the world what hatred, greed, misogyny, a quest for worldly power, a lust for violence, bullying, corruption, and division looks like. A harvest of believers who should have come to know Jesus as Lord has been given a multitude of reasons not to trust the evangelical church in America. This is the cost of choosing power over love. This is the cost of betrayal. This is the Judas Effect.

---

4. 2 Cor 11:3.

Introduction

It has always been my contention that, ultimately, telling the truth is the most important thing the evangelical church can do. I mean, we are out here trying to convince the world that we know the way to God. They aren't going to go anywhere near us, let alone follow us, if we have one foot on the road of truth and the other on a road of lies.

The truth is that the world watched in horror while the church made a spiritual alliance with a fraudulent con artist and abuser. Yes, I said spiritual. It wasn't just a political alliance. Anytime a leader is purported to be "chosen" by God, his supporters are open to being spiritually exploited. This is what happened with Donald Trump. Trump agreed to do what Evangelicals wanted of him, so he was regularly cast by church leaders as King Cyrus, or God's Chosen Candidate. He offered the church everything it ever wanted: political control, protection of religious freedoms, Supreme Court judges—what was not to like? Trump's offer of power created a virtual utopia in the minds of many Evangelicals who had been waiting a long time for things we were sure God wanted us to have. A heaven on earth, if you will. But there is a cost to this type of political expediency, and too many entered into a full-on, unbridled partnership with Trump without counting the cost. Somewhere there is a verse about gaining the whole world at the expense of your soul. If one's soul is the seat of one's integrity and capacity for truth-telling, I'd say the verse applies here.

INTRODUCTION

The Message translation of the Bible uses the term "bully-ruler" to describe a leader who routinely name-calls and oppresses his subjects.[1] It's dangerous for the Christian church to align itself closely with *any* person other than Jesus, but particularly with a bully-ruler like Trump. When Jesus told his disciples to "keep a sharp eye out . . . for the followers of Herod,"[2] he was warning against the temptation of political power that would come through association with a bully-ruler. As we've seen by now, lust for power can completely overtake the people of God. When this happens, the lust becomes a contaminant, like a yeast that multiplies upon itself as it works its way through the whole batch of dough.

I've heard it said in evangelical circles, "You become like that which you worship." By shifting focus off of the nature and character of Christ, and putting it onto a man many believed would "save" their cause, large swaths of the church became more synonymous with Trump than with Christ.

Just prior to the 2016 election, a popular pastor that I used to follow on social media attempted to reassure his followers that Donald Trump was a successful man, and that his success could mean good things for the church if he was elected. His use of the word "successful" stopped me dead in my tracks. I'd never thought of Donald Trump that way. Wealthy? Yes. Powerful? Certainly. Successful? No.

> A joyful heart, thriving in peace? No.
>
> A clear mind, producing clear thoughts, and the capacity to express those thoughts maturely? No.
>
> Self-restraint? No.
>
> The ability to value other people as people, despite differences of opinion? No.
>
> The ability to receive constructive criticism? No.
>
> Possessing a heart that produces both kindness and strength? No.

Eight years later, following a presidential term that ended in chaos and bloodshed due to his refusal to give up power, "success" is still not a word I would ever use to describe a man who may be financially wealthy, but who is so obviously impoverished in spirit. I still see only a tormented and oppressed man. A man who brazenly lies to hold on to power. I see

---

1. Isa 14:5.
2. Mark 8:15.

someone who traffics in manipulation and is also easily manipulated. I see a man whose self-esteem is fragile and whose ego is easily threatened. I see a man who is thirsty for praise and adoration and who demands loyalty above all else. I see a man who lashes out in bursts of anger. I see a man who promotes not just discord but actual violence. I see a man who belittles people because it makes him feel bigger. I see a man who cannot always manage his hands, his mouth, or his emotions. He has admitted that he just can't help himself.[3] He is compelled to grab, compelled to yell, compelled to call people horrible names. So he is a man who is not in control of himself. Which begs the question, if Donald Trump is not in control of Donald Trump, then who is?

I've found that when you pray for someone often enough, you develop a certain affection for them, even if you don't necessarily "like" them or their behavior. After so many years of prayer, I feel almost maternal toward Mr. Trump. He reminds me of a lost little boy trying to pilot his way through the maze of an adult world that is too big for him. The inner compass that most powerful leaders possess, which helps them to navigate the maze and lead others through it, is not working right for Donald. He has a compass that, just when you think it is headed true north, starts spinning around like crazy. So he keeps bumping into things and going in circles, making us all dizzy. He makes me think of the man in the Bible who had the legion of demons. Jesus loved the man. He loved him so much that he addressed the demons.

In my prayer time, I pray for our former president to be at peace, at rest, whole, healthy, and of sound mind. I hope you will join me in that prayer. In the meantime, I don't see how it does followers of Jesus any good to pretend that he was ever a stable, healthy person, or a wise businessman or a strategic politician. For heaven's sake, the world can see right through that facade. No one is fooled. Even so, much of the church seems to want to gloss over his instability, as if we can make it go away by pretending it doesn't exist. But by denying the truth, we give the world—our harvest field—every good reason to distrust us. Going along with Trump's facade may make us feel politically powerful, but it effectively burns our witness to the ground.

Far better to humble ourselves, tell the truth about him, and renounce any Trumpian characteristics with which we inadvertently came into

---

3. "You know, I'm automatically attracted to beautiful—I just start kissing them. It's like a magnet. Just kiss. I don't even wait" (Mark Makela, "Transcript: Donald Trump's Taped Comments about Women," *New York Times*, October 8, 2016, https://www.nytimes.com/2016/10/08/us/donald-trump-tape-transcript.html).

INTRODUCTION

alignment. The characteristics Donald Trump is most known for (found in Ps 10 and Prov 6), include narcissism, arrogance, puffed-up pride, boastfulness, superiority, contempt toward perceived enemies, paranoia, an insatiable hunger to "win" at all costs, a mouth full of curses and lies, harmful words, mocking gestures, divisiveness, violence-provoking, and a refusal to be held accountable.[4] None of these characteristics, obviously, are compatible with Christ, and they should therefore be loudly repudiated by the people who claim his name. As inconvenient as it is for those like myself who lean politically conservative, speaking the truth—and only the truth—about our former president is what this book aims to do. Only the truth will set us free from what was an ill-advised, unholy spiritual alliance with a bully-ruler.

> No doubt about it! God is good—
> > good to good people, good to the good-hearted.
> But I nearly missed it,
> > missed seeing his goodness.
> I was looking the other way,
> > looking up to the people
> At the top,
> > envying the wicked who have it made,
> Who have nothing to worry about,
> > not a care in the whole wide world.
> Pretentious with arrogance,
> > they wear the latest fashions in violence,
> Pampered and overfed,
> > decked out in silk bows of silliness.
> They jeer, using words to kill;
> > they bully their way with words.
> They're full of hot air,
> > loudmouths disturbing the peace.
> People actually listen to them—can you believe it?
> > Like thirsty puppies, they lap up their words.[5]

---

4. See Ps 10 and Prov 6:16–19.
5. Ps 73:1–10.

1

Fly High with Hawk

Steve Hawk and I met in 1984 in junior high, at a school called, coincidentally enough, the Horizon Hawks. We were fourteen. He had a crush on me because I was a cheerleader, and I thought he was cute and distinguished because he won his campaign for ASB president with the unbeatable slogan "Fly High with Hawk!" Unfortunately, high school boundary lines intervened, and we ended up at different high schools. We lost touch until mid-college, when we ran into each other at a cowboy bar in Stateline, Idaho. Between shots of tequila and the "Boot Scootin' Boogie," we reconnected, and the very next day he left his friend's cabin on the Pend Oreille River, where he was supposed to be staying the weekend, and drove two hours to my family cabin on Coeur d'Alene Lake. He told his friend he had to "see about a girl." Steve rolled up to our cabin in his 1990s-era pine-green Subaru with a half-melted gallon of cookie dough ice cream and a winning smile, which immediately won my family over. He also had piercing blue-gray eyes, could do a 360 on the wakeboard, and happily played Clue with my three younger sisters, who were smitten. Even my mom was charmed. Two years later, he proposed, and we made plans for what would be a fairy-tale wedding.

I had my Prince Charming and the shiny ring, now I just needed a royal venue. My heart was set on the enormous, stunningly gorgeous St. John's Episcopal Cathedral on the South Hill in Spokane, Washington. It looked like a real castle, and it would be perfect, but there was just one problem: you had to be a member to be married there. Not only was I *not* a member, I could count on one hand the number of times I had been in a church. My interest in God was virtually nil, but never underestimate the sudden faith arousal of a determined young bride-to-be who has found the perfect venue for her wedding. I decided to become an Episcopalian. I signed up for classes at St. John's, and those classes were my first real introduction to Christian theology. I was twenty-four.

I was worried about what my parents would think about me taking the classes. I knew my mom believed, on some level, in the power of prayer, because there had been a prayer hanging on the wall outside my bedroom door while I was growing up. Inside an ornate gold frame was a picture of a little girl with golden locks kneeling beside her bed. The inscription read, "Now I lay me down to sleep, I pray the Lord my soul to keep. If I should die before I wake, I pray the Lord my soul to take." As I recall, that picture hung there for my entire childhood. But no one in my home had ever actually talked about the sentiment inside the gold frame, or about the Lord who was hopefully going to swoop down and take my soul if by some chance I accidently died while I was sleeping.

I was pretty sure my stepdad did not believe in God or prayer. One time I heard him laughing at a rowdy minister on the TV that he came across while channel surfing. And I had heard both of my parents make disparaging remarks about overly religious people. So I didn't quite know how to tell them I had been going to church. I was relieved when, after several months of me covertly attending St. John's, they came to my confirmation ceremony and met the priest. I remember wanting us all to appear devout, and I was nervous that someone in my family would spill food, or fart, or go completely off road and tell a bad joke and blow my cover. But thankfully, my mom wore a nice dress, my dad wore a suit, and everyone was on their best behavior. I introduced my fiancé to the priest as "Steven," and my dad got a good chuckle out of my sudden formality. We ate the snacks the church provided, shook a lot of hands congratulating me, and I signed a document that said I was a confirmed Episcopalian. But to me, it was simply a ticket that would ensure a beautiful backdrop to my wedding. I had no idea whether or not I actually believed in God. Neither did Steven.

After our wedding, we went along our happily married way, never thinking twice about the commitment I had made to the church in order to use their facilities. A couple of years went by, and we didn't think about God either, until one of Steve's best friends (the one whose cabin he had deserted to come up to mine) invited us to church. We were absolutely floored. These were our best club-hopping buddies, definitely not church-going people. But they had been struggling in their short marriage, and someone had convinced them that God might be able to help. Steve and I didn't think it would work; we were much more for the "let's just keep going out dancing and partying every weekend" save-the-marriage plan, but we loved our friends and decided to join them at our local Presbyterian church in a show of support for their new hobby. Of course, we chose the Saturday night service because it was shorter, only an hour, and we could be out in time to have dinner and hit the dance clubs afterward. This clumsy plan to rescue their marriage went on for several months.

Then something astonishing happened. We joined a couples group with them, which involved doing a Bible study. This meant we had to actually purchase a Bible. Now that this God thing was getting serious, we needed to decide if we really believed. I was busy preparing for our first baby, and Steve had degrees in physics and math, so I assigned him to the task. I figured his scientific mind would break down the myth of Jesus, and we could put this whole experience to rest. But after a few months of Bible study and reading a book called *The Case for Christ*, Steve determined that Jesus really did die on a cross and rose again.[1] Honestly, I couldn't have been more shocked when he slammed the book shut in bed one night, turned to me, and declared that he thought we should believe in Jesus.

Our lives changed dramatically. Neither of us is known for doing anything halfway, and we jumped into church life full speed ahead, much to the suspicion of our families. Besides the couples Bible study group, we joined a men's and women's study separately. We went to every prayer retreat and fellowship camp offered. I served in Adventureland, and Steve became an usher. After our daughter Savanna was born, I worked in the nursery part-time and brought her with me. It was a large church, and I worked there for ten years, becoming a small-groups coach and coordinator, and eventually the women's ministry director. Steve became a Gideon, and then went on to lead the Evangelism Explosion ministry. We were "hungry for the Lord," to use an evangelical term. We couldn't get enough of Jesus.

Every afternoon, while Savanna took her nap, I kneeled on the floor of my closet. Fortunately, it was carpeted, and it was the best place I could find to meet with Jesus. I poured out my heart to him, and when I thought I heard something back, I journaled it. I did Bible study after Bible study,

---

1. Lee Strobel, *The Case for Christ: A Journalist's Personal Investigation of the Evidence for Jesus* (Grand Rapids: Zondervan, 1998).

almost obsessively. Two hours would go by, and I would hear Savanna stirring down the hall in her crib, and I would feel like I was just getting started. I learned through the Scriptures and through a flourishing relationship with a living God that I was special, chosen, adopted, redeemed, and empowered through his Holy Spirit. As a woman who had struggled with insecurity my whole life, it truly was the best news I'd ever heard.

Moreover, I found myself wanting to be like Jesus. I knew I could be impatient, and I prayed for God to change me. Three years after Savanna, our son Cruise was born, and I felt like I was a better, calmer parent because of Jesus's influence. I was traditionally selfish by nature, plotting and planning Steve's rise within his company so that we could afford a bigger house and better cars. Now I found myself wanting to give. Steve and I devoted our finances, our time, and our energy to the church, for the promotion of Christ and his gospel.

At the same time that we were falling in love with Jesus, we were falling in love with the upward trajectory of our leadership positions in the church. In 2002 we traveled to Willow Creek in Chicago to take a discipleship intensive, and over the next decade we made several visits to Bethel Church in Redding, California, to investigate prophetic prayer and healing. Steve took an Evangelism Explosion course in Seattle and then came back and started organizing tract handouts in Riverfront Park. By the time Cruise hit kindergarten, I was leading the women's ministry (I was particularly proud of the name, RefresHER!), coaching new Bible study leaders, and had started a prayer and healing room in an abandoned room upstairs in our church. Our pastor commended us. He said we grew so rapidly we must be on God's fast track to leadership. In ten years' time, we went from not believing in God at all to leading large ministries. We were, as they say in some church circles, "on fire." The Hawks were flying high. We were important in the church, and we knew it.

* * *

With a sense of urgency, Steve and I had set about getting our families saved. To prepare, we took a class called Building the Bridge to God. Steve repeatedly asked his parents and his sister to come to church, to hear the good news, and to see the treasure we had found in Jesus. If one of our children was going to sing or perform on stage, they would come, but the rest of the time it was a polite "no thanks." I had two sets of parents plus my younger sisters and a younger brother to convince. I made my mom come with me to see Beth Moore at the Spokane Convention Center, and she and my sister Laura came with me, albeit reluctantly, to hear Franklin Graham preach at Albi Stadium. It didn't go well. I got in a fight with my mom at Beth Moore and argued with my sister through most of Franklin's sermon. But still, Steve and I were undeterred. It was our duty to share the good news, dammit, even if no one in our immediate circle cared to hear it. After attending a Dave Ramsey conference, I generously gave my younger sister Nikki and her new husband Brett a complete set of Financial Peace University materials, including the workbook and CDs, just in case they wanted to take the course from home. It turned out they didn't.

Then the good Lord provided what we considered to be the most powerful proselytizing tool ever invented. Like manna from heaven, Rick Warren's *The Purpose Driven Life* fell right out of the sky and into our laps, and we devoured it with gusto.[2] Our church responded with a frenzy of activity. As the small-group coordinator, it was my job to put together nearly one hundred community groups to read together and discuss the book. Steve and I promptly signed up to lead a home group, invited our neighbors, and then we bought about twenty copies. We decided for Christmas that year to sit back and let Rick Warren do the work of getting our loved ones saved. All of our parents and every sibling received a carefully wrapped copy of what we felt sure would change their lives and lead them to Christ. But strangely, they didn't act grateful, thankful, *or* blessed. Exasperated, my mom finally told us to stop smothering everybody with Christian materials. Steve and I were genuinely dumbfounded. This wasn't the way they said it would go in the Building the Bridge to God class.

I was especially frustrated with my stepdad, the wisest, most courageous person I knew, and my own personal hero. I had also given him a book called *Letters from a Skeptic*, and he didn't like it.[3] His opinion on any topic, more than anyone else's, meant the world to me. My dad was a former fighter pilot in the Air Force and a prisoner of war in Vietnam. He had survived six years in the Hanoi Hilton and then come back to Spokane, married his high school sweetheart (my mom, who already had two young daughters), and graduated from Gonzaga Law School to become a

---

2. Rick Warren, *The Purpose Driven Life: What on Earth Am I Here For?* (Grand Rapids: Zondervan, 2013), 10th anniv. ed.

3. Gregory A. Boyd and Edward K. Boyd, *Letters from a Skeptic: A Son Wrestles with His Father's Questions about Christianity* (Colorado Springs: David Cook, 1994).

very successful and admired US attorney. His experiences had made him humble and patient and gracious, and his perspective on any given topic was like gold. So it bothered me greatly that we could not see eye to eye on God.

I sat him down one afternoon and tried to explain that it was Jesus who had rescued him from the prison camp. It was because of Jesus that he had survived the war and came home to marry my mom. I wanted him to attend church with me, so he could hear more and believe. He was very polite in his response, but Captain Jim Shively had no use for religion or religious people. His best friend growing up had been a pastor's son. He saw his friend's family behave one way at church and a completely different way at home. As an adult, he'd been scammed in a moneymaking venture by two God-professing business partners. Jim Shively had a keen eye for bullies, and for con artists who hid their greed behind a religious veneer. His experiences with church people were mostly marked by hypocrisy, not-so-subtle bullying, and power grabs, and he told me as much. I carried his warnings in the back of my mind even as I vowed to overcome my family's misconceptions about power-hungry religious folk.

And then Trump happened.

2

Trump Happens

The wind blew us south from Washington to Oregon in the summer of 2010. Steve had become an impressive (read: addicted) windsurfer, and he felt God leading us to the Columbia River Gorge where he could "ride on the wings of the wind"[1] with God anytime he wanted. I followed dutifully, although it was hard to leave our families, our friends, and our church behind. We joined an Assemblies of God church, where I was teaching adult discipleship classes, and Steve sang on the worship team. Although they were only eleven and eight when we moved, we had discovered that Savanna had a beautiful singing voice and Cruise had a special talent on guitar, drums, and bass. The kids occasionally joined the worship team in "big church" and were frequent special musical guests, much to the delight of the grandparents in our congregation, who declared the Hawk children to be "special and holy, set apart for his good works." I wholeheartedly nodded and agreed, glad that none of the sweet grandparents at church had to witness how my "holy" children behaved at home, where rehearsals usually ended with one of them pushing the other off of the piano bench.

Nonetheless, we did everything we could to raise them up for the Lord. My car practically drove itself in the circle from the private Christian school they attended to church to our Bible study community group and back again. I loved it. Church was my life, and I was content in my belief that as a wife and mom and daughter of the Most High King, I was doing

1. Ps 104:3.

everything right. If you had asked me in 2015, I would have told you that the evangelical Christian bubble I was living within was made of the finest steel, with nary a crack, as strong as my faith and love for Jesus.

And I would have been wrong. It was more like a sheer pink, fragile balloon of Bubblicious bubble gum, and I had no idea it was about to pop.

When Donald Trump was elected in 2016, largely due to the evangelical vote, that bubble burst, and everything I'd based my adult life on shattered around it. I was left with gum on my face, embarrassed and confused by the church's triumphant celebration of a man who was not only the antithesis of Jesus, but who represented everything I did not want my son to grow up to be.

The year of our Lord two thousand and sixteen unfolded like a scroll delivered straight from the fiery pit of a chaotic, unrelenting, inexplicable hell. Amidst a nonstop barrage of Twitter assault from the new leader of the free world, I lost sleep, cried for three days, had nightmares, my eyelashes fell out, and I woke up in the night furious at God. The president's gaslighting took a psychological toll that left me alternately despairing and enraged. The abusive tweets, the nonsensical statements, saying one thing one day and denying it the next. The day the president taunted a female journalist by calling her "low I.Q. crazy" and "bleeding badly from a face-lift,"[2] I screamed so loud at the TV I scared the dog, and she went whimpering into the laundry room. Steve and I looked at each other and wondered how on earth this abuse from the White House could even be happening, aided and abetted by people who professed to follow Christ, who should have been the first to publicly rebuke him. For heaven's sake, they rebuked Obama for wearing a tan suit.

Up until the election, I thought I knew what we all stood for. Kindness, integrity, and truth were virtues I could get behind and advertise to the world with confidence. Those were the qualities I wanted my younger siblings to see in me and in the Christian institutions I devoted my life to. I wanted them to be intrigued enough to join the church and meet Jesus in the same way Steve and I had. But the feverish celebration of Donald Trump was the nail in the coffin that dashed those hopes forever. If our fellow Christ followers had been more reserved, if they had been willing

---

2. Donald J. Trump (@realDonaldTrump), "I heard poorly rated @Morning_Joe," Twitter, June 29, 2017, 5:52 a.m., https://twitter.com/realDonaldTrump/status/880408582310776832; Donald J. Trump (@realDonaldTrump), ". . . to Mar-a-Lago 3 nights," Twitter, June 29, 2017, 5:58 a.m., https://twitter.com/realDonaldTrump/status/880410114456465411.

to rebuke him when it was so regularly and obviously called for, we could have dealt better with their praise of him, understanding the weight that a potential Roe v. Wade reversal carried to the Christian voter. Instead, to our great dismay, well-known leaders, some we had trusted for years, repeatedly swept Trump's abuses under the rug, or worse, excused his outright lies. It was a betrayal of everything the church had previously taught us. We questioned the kind of church that would defend a man who bragged about sexual assault, refused to disclose his tax returns, called women names, and bullied people regularly. A Jesus-following church wouldn't—but a cult would. White, Americanized Evangelicalism was looking more like a cult every day. And Trump was its leader.

I had been taught in church that "the world" could not be trusted to see things clearly, because they didn't have the Holy Spirit to guide them. But in the case of Trump, the world was not deceived. They saw very clearly who he was, precisely because they believed what they saw and heard, with their own eyes and ears, unfiltered, in real time. Meanwhile, Christian conservatives seemed to be wearing glasses and hearing aids that filtered everything he said and did through the lens of how it benefited their political interests. When Trump mimicked a physically disabled journalist and a physically disabled senator, they couldn't see it. When he paid money to a porn star to try to keep her quiet, they pretended not to know it. When he solicited a foreign country to interfere in our elections, they couldn't hear it. The values I loved most about the church I adored went flying out the window in its refusal to acknowledge basic truth. Morality, dignity, and integrity—sold to the highest bidder. Trump promised to give the evangelical church the whole damn world, everything they ever wanted, but for Steve and me, the soul went out of it.

I'd made my home-away-from-home in the pews for nearly twenty years, attending and serving multiple times a week, but now church ceased to be a place where I found peace. It felt scratchy and uncomfortable and phony. I no longer trusted the judgment of anyone touting Trump, which caused me to rethink everything I'd ever been taught. Even during worship, I realized I didn't "feel" the presence of Jesus in the same way. It was like the cloudy pillar had moved on, and I couldn't wait to move on with it. We determined we needed a break from the evangelical bubble, but we didn't want to be hasty. Steve continued on the worship team, and I was serving a three-year term on the elder board, an elected position and one I felt honored to be in. We also greatly appreciated our pastor, who understood, to some degree, how we felt. Besides, as uncomfortable as we were with Trumpism, we had many friends in our congregation, although judging by their Facebook posts, we had less and less in common with them all the time. We decided to "pray it through" until God made our steps clear.

One Sunday morning I listened intently as a fellow congregant took the stage and sang of God's grace. In the song, the Lord opened up his hands to receive her in any condition, as soon as she knocked on his door. She brought all her pain and cares to him and laid them at his feet, and he welcomed her with loving arms of comfort. She sang about his unending love and care, which was available to anyone at any time. I cried, but not because I was moved by her song. I cried because I had read her Facebook post that morning. That very morning, she had disparaged immigrants at the border, and commended taking their children away. Apparently, her God was big enough to care for her in her every distress but was not big enough for mothers fleeing violence and seeking a better life for their children. She could conceive that God would call her out of *her* troubles and guide *her* to safety, but the very same God wouldn't do that for a courageous immigrant family. (Even though God did exactly that in Matt 2.)

It dawned on me then. We went to church together every week. We listened to the same sermons. We sang the same songs. We read the same Bible. But we were following different gods. I was following the God who was adamant about treating immigrants with courtesy and respect. The evangelical church had taught me that, "God defends the cause of the fatherless and the widow, and loves the foreigner residing among you, giving them food and clothing. And you are to love those who are foreigners, for you yourselves were foreigners in Egypt."[3] And, "When a stranger sojourns with you in your land, you shall not do him wrong."[4] Jesus said, "For I was hungry and you gave me food, I was thirsty and you gave me drink, I was a stranger and you welcomed me."[5] The god she was following, who encouraged her to belittle and mistreat immigrants, didn't sound much like Jesus to me. In her Facebook post, he sounded a heck of a lot like Tucker Carlson.

A short time later, our church had a guest speaker, commended by the regional governing body of Assemblies of God, who came to teach us his foolproof method of "getting people saved." He took the stage, having never set foot in our congregation before, grabbed the microphone, and

3. Deut 10:18–19 NIV.
4. Lev 19:33 ESV.
5. Matt 25:35 ESV.

told us God had seen fit to use him mightily as he had personally led over one hundred people to salvation just that year. And what a year it had been, he mused, what with the crazy Democrats trying to impeach our godly president for no reason. He went on and on, and I never got to hear about his foolproof methods because I walked out before I vomited all over the chair in front of me. God had made it clear: Steve and I no longer fit in with our local Assembly of God community. It was time to leave.

As I wrote a goodbye letter to our pastor and elder team, I reflected on the weird twist my journey with God had taken. For a long time, I saw the church's role as central to my relationship with Jesus. I thought that I stumbled into it quite by accident, and the nice people there had led me to Christ. Now, I saw my faith story differently. Jesus himself had been pursuing and guiding me since the day I was born. In 1999, he led me into the evangelical church.

In 2020, I followed him out.

3

False Messiah

Watch out for doomsday deceivers. Many leaders are going to show up with forged identities, claiming, "I am Christ, the Messiah." They will deceive a lot of people. —Matt 24:4–5

"I'm the only one!" Donald Trump announced from a stage during a 2016 campaign rally in Pennsylvania—and my spidey senses went into overdrive. There were a lot of reasons already not to like the guy, but hey, I was a traditional Republican with traditional views. I could overlook some bad qualities as long as our candidate delivered on his conservative promises. This particular pronouncement—just a slight variation on the claim Christ made about himself—was probably my first big red flag that something was wrong. And when I say red flag, it was more like every red flag, alarm bell, and whistle went off in my spirit at once. "I'm the only one who can protect you!" Trump boldly claimed, again.[1]

No, sir. Nope. I shook my head and tried to explain to him through the television, "There is only one Lord and one Savior, sir. And you are not him!" But he must not have heard me because during the course of his campaign and beyond, like a broken record, Trump repeated a variation of this grandiose claim with sickening regularity. Every time he said it, it was jarring. It became clear his words were no accident. And those words were

---

1. Steve Benen, "Trump Says He's 'the Only One' Who Can Protect the U.S," MSNBC, October 12, 2016, para. 2, https://www.msnbc.com/rachel-maddow-show/trump-says-hes-the-only-one-who-can-protect-the-us-msna912406.

lodging themselves into the spirits of his evangelical cheerleaders, who became more and more convinced that Trump really was "God's chosen."

"I'm the only one who can fix our problems."[2]

"I'm the only one that matters."[3]

"I alone can fix it."[4]

"I am the chosen one."[5]

Trump's language was explained away by some in the evangelical community as relatively harmless—as if it revealed nothing more than a childishly inflated view of self-importance. And that may be true, from a strictly psychological standpoint. But from a spiritual standpoint, his repeated self-proclamations were no joke. He was using the language of a false messiah. Repetition works. Donald Trump's continual declarations about himself achieved for him exactly what he wanted them to achieve. Only a person under a strong spiritual delusion would dare repeatedly utter those words, from a platform, in front of a large crowd, to an entire country, about himself. And only a powerful spiritual delusion would hold true Christ followers hostage to such a blatant pseudo-christ.[6]

Evangelicals for Trump

"We put God right at the center of the White House," declared televangelist and ardent Trump supporter Paula White, to a roomful of worshipers at

---

2. "Trump: I'm the Only One Who Can Fix Our Problems," CNBC, June 22, 2016, https://www.cnbc.com/video/2016/06/22/trump-im-the-only-one-who-can-fix-our-problems.html.

3. *Don Lemon Tonight*, "Trump: I'm the Only One that Matters," CNN, November 3, 2017, https://www.cnn.com/videos/politics/2017/11/03/trump-im-only-one-that-matters-fox-sot.cnn.

4. Yoni Appelbaum, "I Alone Can Fix It," *Atlantic*, July 21, 2016, para. 7, https://www.theatlantic.com/politics/archive/2016/07/trump-rnc-speech-alone-fix-it/492557/.

5. "President Trump: 'I Am the Chosen One,'" BBC, August 21, 2019, 00:49, https://www.bbc.com/news/av/world-us-canada-49429661.

6. From the Greek word *pseudochristos*—a spurious messiah (Matt 24:24; Mark 13:22), Strongs #5580. "The false christ does not necessarily deny the existence of Christ. On the contrary, he builds on the world's expectations of such a person, while he blasphemously appropriates these to himself and affirms that he is the foretold One in whom God's promises and the Saint's expectations are fulfilled" ("Pseudochristos," in Spiros Zodhiates, ed., *NASB Hebrew-Greek Key Word Study Bible* [Chattanooga: AMG, 2008], rev. ed., 2315).

an event called Evangelicals for Trump.[7] Celebrity Evangelicals Franklin Graham, Jerry Falwell Jr., and Pastor Robert Jeffress agreed. Jeffress went so far as to call Christians who refused to vote for Trump "spineless morons."[8] I recoiled at his insult. Certainly Pastor Jeffress knew that God is not reliant on any one man in order to see his will done on earth . . . especially not one with such character deficits as incessant name-calling and serial lying. (It takes more of a spine to stand up to a bully than it does to bow down to one, Mr. Jeffress.) But by then Donald Trump had not only declared himself their savior; he had also mastered the art of pandering to celebrity Evangelicals for their support, and they responded in kind for his power. It struck me as a kind of devil's bargain, whereby Donald got the praise, glory, and power he had always yearned for, and the church leaders got what they wanted, but God himself was not in on the deal.

In her book *Unholy: Why White Evangelicals Worship at the Altar of Donald Trump*, Sarah Posner observes, "Trump . . . did not just deliver policy, in a quid pro quo with a voting bloc that fueled his election. He delivered power. And for that, he was not merely a reliable politician worthy of their praise. For the Christian right, Trump is no ordinary politician and no ordinary president. He is anointed, chosen, and sanctified by the movement as a divine leader sent by God to save America."[9] Posner's chilling assessment points to a much bigger problem in the church. It suggests a large portion is willing to make a spiritual partnership with a man selling snake oil. Many liked what he had to say so much that they convinced themselves and others that God put him there, despite the many obvious warnings and cautionary Scriptures evincing otherwise.

And God did warn us in advance of the election. We saw the video of Trump physically mocking the disabled reporter. We heard him brag about sexual assault. We witnessed his "win-by-calling-people-names" campaign strategy. To be sure, all of us are sinners in need of God's abundant grace.

---

7. Scott Wartman, "Trump's Minister Rallies Cincinnati Evangelicals: 'We Put God Right at the Center of the White House,'" *Cincinnati Enquirer*, Mar 6, 2020, para. 10, https://www.cincinnati.com/story/news/politics/2020/03/06/trumps-spiritual-adviser-paula-white-rallies-evangelicals-region/4927560002/.

8. Stephen Young, "Robert Jeffress: Christians Who Don't Back Trump Are Morons, Like Christians in Nazi Germany," *Dallas Observer*, February 13, 2019, para. 3, https://www.dallasobserver.com/news/dallas-pastor-robet-jeffress-says-anti-trump-christians-are-morons-11561290.

9. Sarah Posner, *Unholy: Why White Evangelicals Worship at the Altar of Donald Trump* (New York: Random House, 2020), 8.

But a person who persists in abusive behavior and divisiveness, who makes a lifestyle out of bullying people, and who has never expressed one iota of regret or remorse, is never called to lead. Rather than embrace such a person as a leader, the Bible cautions us to steer clear.

> Reject a divisive person after one or two warnings. You know that such a person is twisted by sin and is conscious of it himself.[10]

> Now the works of the flesh are obvious: sexual immorality, impurity, depravity, idolatry, sorcery, hostilities, strife, jealousy, outbursts of anger, selfish rivalries, dissensions, factions, envying, murder, drunkenness, carousing, and similar things. I am warning you, as I had warned you before: Those who practice such things will not inherit the kingdom of God![11]

Donald Trump was never "anointed, chosen, and sanctified" by God. Had he been, we would have seen a repentant heart, rather than a heart set on bullying and name-calling and divisiveness. According to Scripture, we should be even more wary if a boastful, routinely abusive person suddenly becomes religious or makes an alignment with religious people at a strategic time in his life at which to prosper himself:

> But understand this, that in the last days difficult times will come. For people will be lovers of themselves, lovers of money, boastful, arrogant, blasphemers, disobedient to parents, ungrateful, unholy, unloving, irreconcilable, slanderers, without self-control, savage, opposed to what is good, treacherous, reckless, conceited, loving pleasure rather than loving God. They will maintain the outward appearance of religion but will have repudiated its power. So avoid people like these.[12]

Trump did not possess the grace of God in his rise to the top. What Trump possessed is a boastful, self-exalting spirit that worked overtime to catapult him to high places. He did not care who he hurt on the way up. He did not care who he disparaged. He did not care who he mocked. He did not care who he stole from. He did not care how many lies he had to tell or conspiracy theories he had to circulate to get there. He did not care how many women he had to pay off. He got there, but he got there void of God's help. We know this because if one elevates oneself to a

---

10. Titus 3:10–11 NET.
11. Gal 5:19–21 NET.
12. 2 Tim 3:1 NET.

high position through abusive and deceptive and exploitative means, the power obtained once there is not from God.

Regardless, Trump knew who elected him and absolutely reveled in their praise. His blasphemous claims had become so commonplace by 2021, it hardly registered as a shock when he asserted, "Nobody has done more for Christianity, or for evangelicals, or for religion itself, than I have."[13] Insecure people, especially, like to be praised. They'll do whatever it takes to keep it coming. But Evangelicals should never praise a person for his high status while at the same time showing utter disregard for his gross misbehavior. A good rule of thumb when assessing a leader in *any* area is to heed Jesus's own advice about such hypocrisy:

> Be careful about following *them*. They talk a good line, but they don't live it. They don't take it into their hearts and live it out in their behavior. It's all spit-and-polish veneer. . . . Their lives are perpetual fashion shows, embroidered prayer shawls one day and flowery prayers the next. They love to sit at the head table at church dinners, basking in the most prominent positions, preening in the radiance of public flattery, receiving honorary degrees, and getting called "Doctor" and "Reverend."[14]

(Or, in Trump's case, "Mr. President.")

While the leaders on Trump's evangelical council flattered him as "God's chosen," their false messiah basked in the glory of their praise . . . and happily signed whatever document they put in front of him.

Cult of Personality

Leah Remini's documentary *Scientology and the Aftermath* came out shortly after Trump's inauguration.[15] I was obsessed. Every Tuesday night I hushed my family at 8 p.m. sharp, snuggled into the couch with my favorite blanket, and tuned into A&E for the latest breathtaking installment. Every single episode brought me to incredulous tears. Scientologists adamantly believe that it is their religion alone that will save the world, and

---

13. Marcus Jones, "Donald Trump: 'Nobody Has Done More for Christianity than I Have,'" *Premier Christian News*, October 1, 2021, para. 3, https://premierchristian.news/en/news/article/donald-trump-nobody-has-done-more-for-christianity-than-i-have.

14. Matt 23:2–7; emphasis original.

15. Leah Remini and Mike Rinder, presenters, *Leah Remini: Scientology and the Aftermath*, released November 29, 2016—August 26, 2019, on A&E.

it is because of this belief that they put up with abuse from their leader. The CEO's wife has been missing since August 2007, with no explanation from the church. Some Scientologists have been manipulated into going completely bankrupt to fund their church's world-saving mission. Sexual abuse is rampant. Members of the church who refuse to comply with its rules are sent to a barbed-wire-enclosed prison camp, and there is a labor camp where they "train" young children to be Scientologists—away from the care of their parents. Members of Scientology who leave the group are shunned and labeled "suppressive." I was fascinated by what made Scientologists join in the first place, but mostly I was intrigued by the large personality of the man who held them there.

David Miscavige, the CEO of Scientology following the death of L. Ron Hubbard, is charismatic, energetic, and commands attention. Out front, he greets his parishioners in a charming and effusive manner. But behind the scenes, he is a ruthless authoritarian—abusive, demanding, and controlling. People are expendable to him, and those closest to him know better than to cross him. He is excessively wealthy. His organization does not pay taxes. He despises the news media and, unless it is something positive written about Scientology, declares it fake news and commands his flock not to read it. He swindles, bullies, and lies, but because he preaches a good message and declares himself to be the one and only man capable of leading them, his followers are fiercely protective, even as they excuse his abusiveness. He can act very devout when it suits him. David Miscavige is attracted to power, craves continual praise and undying loyalty, threatens anyone who gets in his way, and is hiding behind a "religion" to promote himself. Scientology's parishioners enable him because they believe that under his leadership good things are happening in the world that make his sketchy misbehavior worth it in the end.

Watching *Scientology* sparked my interest in how cults operate. I watched *Wild Wild Country*, *Waco: Madman or Messiah*, *The Vow*, and *Seduced: Inside the NXIVM Cult*.[16] I read Catherine Oxenberg's heartbreaking book detailing her daughter's rescue out of NXIVM.[17] I read Elizabeth Es-

---

16. Maclain Way and Chapman Way, dirs., *Wild Wild Country*, released March 16, 2018, on Netflix; Christopher Spencer, dir., *Waco: Madman or Messiah*, released January 28–29, 2018, on A&E; Jehane Noujaim et al., producers, *The Vow*, released August 23, 2020–November 21, 2022, on HBO; Cecilia Peck and Inbal B. Lessner, *Seduced: Inside the NXIVM Cult*, released October 18–November 8, 2020, on Starz.

17. Catherine Oxenberg with Natasha Stoynoff, *Captive: A Mother's Crusade to Save Her Daughter from a Terrifying Cult* (New York: Gallery, 2018).

ther's memoir, *Girl at the End of the World*, about growing up in the fundamentalist Christian cult her grandfather started.[18] I read *Under the Banner of Heaven*, *Educated*, and *The Polygamist's Daughter*.[19] They all have striking similarities. Within each organization, the world outside is positioned as a radical and scary place. This creates a mental prison for the followers, who are trained to believe that the only "safe" place for them is within the confines of their religion or institution. Within each organization, there are leaders who routinely downplay the importance of emotions, so that parishioners are taught over time that their feelings, and the feelings of other people, don't really matter. This indoctrination allows for bullying, mocking, and intimidation techniques to be used without question.

In every cult I studied, the leader was abusive but still able to attract thousands of members. The leader acted piously when the situation called for it, praying and receiving prayer, and he also managed to convince his parishioners that he was specially appointed by a higher authority and the "only one" capable of leading them toward society's greater good. The end result, as explained by cult experts Janja Lalich and Madeline Tobias, is that his supporters "displayed excessively zealous and unquestioning commitment to their leader, regardless of his outward behavior."[20]

* * *

It was while attending an evangelical church that I learned that Jesus had a very special spiritual empowerment that allowed him to carry out his earthly ministry. This holy anointing from God drew people to him in an extraordinary way. Jesus said, "Come, follow me," and they did. Crowds chased after him, pressing in on all sides.

There is a counterfeit version of the "Come, follow me" empowerment. A person with this counterfeit anointing is what the Bible calls a false leader or messiah. A false messiah carries a certain charisma that people want to follow, but he is leading them nowhere good. It is effective

---

18. Elizabeth Esther, *Girl at the End of the World: My Escape from Fundamentalism in Search of Faith with a Future* (New York: Random House, 2014).

19 Jon Krakauer, *Under the Banner of Heaven: A Story of Violent Faith* (New York: Random House, 2003); Tara Westover, *Educated: A Memoir* (New York: Random House, 2018); Anna LeBaron with Leslie Wilson, *The Polygamist's Daughter: A Memoir* (Carol Stream, IL: Tyndale Momentum, 2017).

20. Janja Lalich and Madeline Tobias, *Take Back Your Life: Recovering from Cults and Abusive Relationships* (Richmond: Bay Tree, 2006), 2nd ed., 327–28.

because it hides behind a moral agenda at the same time it uses bullying, exploitation, and abuse tactics to achieve said agenda. Dangerous men like L. Ron Hubbard, David Miscavige, Keith Raniere, Jim Jones, and David Koresh are examples of dynamic leaders who captivated multitudes, demanded loyalty, refused correction, convinced their parishioners never to believe anything bad written about them, and whose abusive authority went remarkably unquestioned among the people they led. In all cases, the leader became something of an idol, rather than a person held to the same standards of behavior one would expect from anyone else. In all cases, the followers made a profound spiritual commitment to their leader, believing him ultimately to be led by God, or a higher power.

To some Evangelicals, it was okay that Trump attacked women, called people names, told obnoxious lies on the regular, was abusive and incoherent, wouldn't willingly release his tax forms, initially sidestepped the denunciation of white supremacy and Nazism, told his supporters to go ahead and "rough them up" at rallies, mocked the disabled, disparaged war heroes, and incited violence toward the free press. They were able to justify it, because in the end, they believed he had a moral agenda for America. Donald Trump stood in front of a church with a Bible, so it was all good. "Believe me," he kept repeating, over and over, "I'm the only one." He told them Vladimir Putin was someone to be admired, and they believed him. He told them that any news that criticized him was fake, and they believed him. He told them that the 2020 election was "rigged and stolen." And they believed him.

There is no greater distortion to the true gospel of Christ than to hold up a leader who bullies, lies, threatens, and promotes violence, and assert that God appointed him. A church that exalts any leader—political, religious, or otherwise—who regularly stirs up division and violence, unleashes anger and hatred, lies incessantly, threatens reporters, and belittles women, is not a church. It's a cult.

"Come, follow me," said Donald Trump. And Evangelicals did.

4

Never Bow to a Bully

Who knows what bullies think, or if they even think? Bullies are people who use conflict as a means for obtaining power. Some young people grow out of this; others don't and become old bullies.—Bob Goff, *Love Does*[1]

"What are you, stupid? Were you born at Kmart?" I was tormented in the fifth grade. It was the 1980s, and I can still see his scowling face, curly brown mullet, and the "Frankie Says Relax" T-shirt he always wore. He was a couple of years older than me and huge for his age. My best friend Natalie and I tried to shrink ourselves and meld into our seats when he came onto the bus. We prayed he wouldn't sit behind us, but we were easy targets, small and studious, clutching our Lisa Frank sticker books. When the bully wasn't there, our bus ride home was sublime. Thirty minutes alone to compare our latest sticker acquisitions and sometimes trade them—sparkling horses and stars and rainbows and unicorns and butterflies. But when the bus bully was there, the bus was a miserable cavern of darkness and fear. Natalie and I felt sorry for whichever poor shamed soul he happened to pick on that day, but we never spoke up. Best not to draw attention to ourselves. I went home with a stomachache on bully days.

---

1. Bob Goff, *Love Does: Discover a Secretly Incredible Life in an Ordinary World* (Nashville: Thomas Nelson, 2012), 189.

On this day, the poor shamed souls were ours. He threw his backpack and himself into the empty seat behind us. We stayed small and looked out the window, knowing that if we spoke he would jeer over the seat and make stupid comments. He tried to engage us in conversation about the stickers, but we knew from experience we were being baited so we ignored him. He didn't like being ignored. To get a laugh from his bus full of listeners, he said something loudly about the unicorn shoving a star up the horse's butt.

A few people snickered, so he got louder and louder. Natalie's stop came and she got off, and I was alone. I shrank down in my seat, wishing he would turn his attention to someone else. He didn't. When I failed to respond to him, he partially stood up and started leaning over my seat, calling me names, loud enough for the whole bus to hear. I was humiliated. All of my friends were listening. For some reason, I was ashamed. His words were like a poison injection into my soul. Like if he called me stupid, it meant I *was* stupid. And being born at Kmart, well, I couldn't think of a worse insult. My face turned bright red, and there was a sort of panicky squeezing in my chest. I hadn't done anything wrong, why was this happening to me? I sat silent, low in my seat, clutching my sticker book, the contents of which seemed dumb now.

The next stop, thankfully, was mine. I stood up to get off, but something stopped me in my tracks. I slowly turned around and faced him. There was a new feeling in the pit of my stomach, and this time it wasn't shame. It was anger. He was standing, too, and he was taller and bigger than me, but I rose up on my toes, tilted up my chin, and looked him square in the eyes. While the entire bus gaped at us, I lifted my voice to my accuser, and I yelled right into his surprised face, "*Up yours!*" And then I turned and ran off the bus.

He never bothered me again.

Apparently my outburst caused quite a stir, because my mom got a call from one of our neighbors that night, whose son had been there, and she told my mom that I had stood up to the bus bully. Everyone was talking about it. My mom and dad were proud. The ten-year-old inside of me still hates bullying. God doesn't like it, either.

Why be a bully?

"Why not?" you say.

Because God can't stand twisted souls.

—Prov 3:30–31

"Blood Coming Out of Her . . . Wherever"

I could write about Donald Trump's whole sordid and well-documented history of bullying, but it would take this entire book. Suffice to say that his mean streak goes back to childhood, when he pushed a neighbor kid off his bike, threw rocks at a baby in a playpen, called his high school date a "dog," and tried to push his college roommate out of a window.[2]

As a business owner in the eighties and nineties, Trump was known for temper tantrums. He ripped the door off of a cabinet and threw it on the ground when it wouldn't close right, and he screamed expletives at his construction manager when he decided he didn't like a certain marble countertop (that he himself had picked out).[3] Fast-forward to 2023, and every political opponent, as well as any reporter who dares to tell the truth or criticize him, has been a target. Like the bully on the bus, Trump harasses and name-calls relentlessly. "Monster," "nasty," "low-I.Q.," "crazy," "third-rate," "pencil-neck," "creepy," and "sleepy" are just some of the favorites in his repertoire. He has been known to stand closely behind people and leer as a form of intimidation. Another tactic, as confirmed by reporter Katy Tur and her cameraman when it happened to Katy, is to grab a woman unsolicited and kiss her.[4] He called his national security team, which included Rex Tillerson and General James Mattis, "losers, dopes and babies" when they attempted to educate him on matters of diplomacy and military strategy.[5] As recently as January 2023, in an undeniably racist slur, Trump referred to Elaine Chao as "Coco Chow," and to Mitch McConnell as "the Old Broken Crow."[6] It seems nothing is off limits to Trump

---

2. Michael Kranish and Marc Fisher, *Trump Revealed: An American Journey of Ambition, Ego, Money, and Power* (New York: Scribner, 2016), 33–42.

3. David Choi, "'This Is Cheap S—! Who Told You to Buy This?': Trump Went Apoplectic against a Hotel Executive for Installing Cheap Marble That He Chose Himself," *Business Insider*, January 21, 2020, https://www.businessinsider.com/trump-plaza-hotel-marble-executive-very-stable-genius-2020-1.

4. Katy Tur, *Unbelievable: My Front Row Seat to the Craziest Campaign in American History* (New York: HarperCollins, 2017), 54–55.

5. Tom Porter, "Trump Called Top National-Security Officials 'Losers,' 'Dopes and Babies,'" *Business Insider*, January 17, 2020, https://www.businessinsider.com/trump-national-security-meeting-called-officials-losers-dopes-babies-book-2020-1.

6. Matthew Loh, "Elaine Chao, Trump-Era Transportation Secretary and Mitch McConnell's Wife, Hits Back at Trump for Giving Her the Racist Nickname 'Coco Chow,'" *Business Insider*, January 26, 2023, https://www.businessinsider.com/elaine-chao-trump-racist-nickname-coco-chow-response-2023-1.

when he wants to intimidate someone into silence, and his verbal attacks often lead to threats to their physical safety.

Every example of his abuse is unsettling, but maybe none are as disturbing as his harassment of Megyn Kelly, which resulted in her having to hire multiple bodyguards for herself and her family. In *Settle for More*, she describes it as the "Year of Trump," because his relentless cyberbullying took over her life.[7] After years of wooing her with gifts for positive news coverage, Trump found out she couldn't be bought when Ms. Kelly asked him a tough debate question pertaining to his longtime verbal abuse against women. You'd think that the question itself would have made him rethink his treatment of women—but no, instead he threatened to unleash his "beautiful Twitter account" against her, launching a campaign that could only be described as sick and disturbed.[8] He retweeted followers who called her names—"overrated," "angry," and "bimbo"—and attacked her personally, saying she was "not very good or professional," and that she "really bombed."[9]

Trump also apparently has a "thing" about women and blood. He accused Mika Brzezinski of "bleeding badly from a face-lift,"[10] and then said about Megyn Kelly, in a live on-air interview on CNN, "So she gets out there and she starts asking me all sorts of ridiculous questions and you could see the blood coming out of her eyes, blood coming out of her . . . wherever."[11]

"We Can Gut Her"

Trump's comment about Megyn Kelly's blood opened a floodgate of abuse from his more rabid followers, who followed suit by calling her "cunt," "slut," "bitch," and "whore."[12] Prominent politicians on both sides of the aisle called for Trump to drop out of the race. He refused. In fact, instead of stopping the escalation, he kept it going. The online abuse was serving

---

7. Megyn Kelly, *Settle for More* (New York: HarperCollins, 2016), 282.
8. Kelly, *Settle for More*, 244.
9. Kelly, *Settle for More*, 254.
10. Donald J. Trump (@realDonaldTrump), ". . . to Mar-a-Lago 3 nights," Twitter, June 29, 2017, 5:58 a.m., https://twitter.com/realDonaldTrump/status/880410114456465411.
11. Kelly, *Settle for More*, 256–57.
12. Kelly, *Settle for More*, 283.

his purpose of terrorizing Megyn, but it was also sending a signal to other reporters: "Don't mess with Trump."

Over the next year, Trump tweeted 117 messages about Ms. Kelly, calling her "bimbo," "terrible," "unfair," and a "lightweight." He claimed she was "crazy," and without her coverage of him, "her ratings would totally tank."[13] According to Donald Trump, she was "low rated" (not true) and no one had ever heard of her before he came along (also untrue). He lied, saying that he had never sent her anything. (Some of the signed notes, cards, and articles he sent her prior to the debates, when he was trying to win her affection, appear in her book.)[14] His sick obsession with her led to death threats, retweeted by his then lawyer, Michael Cohen. "Fucking die, bitch," "if I see you, you better run!," and "#boycottmegynkelly @realDonaldTrump we can gut her."[15]

He canceled the second debate at the last minute, when his threats couldn't get her to drop out. At the third debate, in Detroit, in March 2016, Megyn asked Donald Trump about Trump University. Her question was more than fair. At the time, Trump was being sued for class-action fraud, and the school had a D-minus rating from the Better Business Bureau. As you can imagine, he didn't like her question. A few days later, he retaliated: "Crazy @megynkelly is unwatchable. Can't watch Crazy Megyn anymore."[16] A new bomb went off. His supporters lashed out, "Fuck off, you slut, I will beat you up so bad I will force you to support trump you slut," "This whore @megynkelly will get hers," "YOU BITCH! . . . twisted bitch, you LOSE, Trump WINS."[17] Again, the intense backlash resulted in more stress, more Fox strategy meetings, aggressive paparazzi, nasty face-to-face encounters with Trump supporters, her husband almost getting beaten up, strange men contacting Megyn's extended family trying to hunt her down, and of course, heightened security. The attacks became so frequent, she was forced to consider the possibility of physical harm coming to one of her children.[18] Her young daughter told her, "I'm afraid of Donald Trump. He wants to

---

13. Kelly, *Settle for More*, 272.
14. Kelly, *Settle for More*, 272.
15. Kelly, *Settle for More*, 262.
16. Kelly, *Settle for More*, 282.
17. Kelly, *Settle for More*, 283.
18. Kelly, *Settle for More*, 282.

hurt me." Kelly promised her that he didn't. Days later she asked, "Mommy, what's a bimbo?"[19] More armed guards were hired.

All because she did her job. She shone a light on the truth about Trump University and Trump's treatment of women, and he didn't like it. He first tried to woo her for positive coverage, when that didn't work he tried to control the debate questions, when that failed he went to the higher-ups at Fox to have her pulled, when that didn't work he made threats through his campaign manager, and when none of that worked, he punished her.

* * *

One of my favorite things about my early experience in the evangelical world was that they seemingly took a hard stand against bullying. Pharaoh was a bully, and God was against him. Nebuchadnezzar, Judas, and Saul were all deemed bullies whose ugly behavior was condemned. The Christian school where I sent my children advertised kindness as one of its core values, claiming that one of the reasons parents should send their children to school there was to get them away from bullying in the public schools. But when I approached our principal to let him know that I didn't think he should be touting Trump, my concerns were dismissed in favor of "getting everything we want" politically.

Evangelicals' sudden laissez-faire attitude about bullying made Steve and me feel like we were living in the upside-down world. People defend bullies either because they are afraid of them outright, or they don't want to lose the position of power that maintaining a friendship affords them. It seemed to us that many in the evangelical church wanted power more than they wanted to accurately represent Christ.

I was taught in church that Jesus is the full and complete revelation of God, and his love is never ending. He is never abusive or mean, therefore those attitudes could not possibly be employed on a regular basis by someone he was "using" to make America more of a "Christian" nation. And if bullying was being tolerated, celebrated, and even copied among those who profess Christ, it made sense that whatever kingdom they thought they were prospering, it had nothing whatsoever to do with Jesus. A refusal to speak out against a bully reveals a willingness to comply with his tactics. But it was in an evangelical church that I learned that God is always on the side of the oppressed.

19. Kelly, *Settle for More*, 279.

> It's true that God is all-powerful, but he doesn't bully innocent people. For the wicked, though, it's a different story—he doesn't give them the time of day, but champions the rights of their victims.[20]

Donald Trump's penchant for cyber abuse didn't start with Megyn Kelly, and it didn't end with her, either. It continued right on through his presidency, extending to Mika Brzezinski, Kamala Harris, Carmen Yulín Cruz, Gretchen Whitmer, Greta Thunberg, Elizabeth Warren, Elaine Chao, and Yamiche Alcindor, to name just a small few. And when he called them names and belittled them, he unleashed every misogynistic demon from hell. His copycat Twitter minions came out of the woodwork to follow his lead, even going so far as to threaten the lives of any woman who dared criticize Donald Trump. It was sickening to watch, but what made it even worse was that many Evangelicals in our midst either chose to ignore it, to downplay it by saying something like "Well, Twitter is crazy," or to actually blame the women. Some said, "Let's keep the president in our prayers," as if lack of prayer was responsible for the president's mean-spiritedness.

Another odd thing happened: some of the nicest Christians I had ever met face-to-face suddenly became bullies online. They called people "libtards" and "snowflakes" for speaking out against Trump's abuse, which was something they, as disciples of Christ, should have been doing. Blinded by power, Evangelicals' personal alliance with Trump infected those who continued to celebrate and embrace his madness.

* * *

One Sunday morning, after a weeklong, particularly brutal round of Trump's cyberbullying, I listened online to one of my favorite preachers. I knew he was a Trump supporter, but as a humble and wise man of God, I felt certain he would condemn the president's recent behavior. It couldn't be avoided; everyone on social media was talking about it. He didn't. He stood at his pulpit and pulled some verse out of Revelation and twisted it to claim that followers of Christ should never speak ill of anyone in a position of leadership. I was crushed.

I wished more evangelical leaders would do what I had done in the fifth grade: stand up and rebuke the bully. A church that defers to a bully is a church the world should never trust. Likewise, a church that stands

---

20. Job 36:5.

up to reprimand him, loudly and clearly, is on the right side of God. But the message from some of the evangelical leaders we had looked up to for many years was loud and clear, and it didn't sound at all like Jesus. Instead, it said, "Don't mess with Trump."

The Hanoi Hilton

I know I talk about my dad a lot, but it's because I'm proud of him. He was a fighter pilot who was shot down over Hanoi on his sixty-ninth mission, at the ripe old age of twenty-four. He parachuted out of his F-105 into a rice paddy and was eventually captured by the North Vietnamese Army. The violence he endured over the next six years is indescribable. He was blindfolded, stripped, beaten, and forced to march through the streets while villagers threw rocks and farm implements at him. He was starved, tortured with ropes, held captive by iron stocks, and humiliated. For six years he used a bucket for his bodily waste, and bowed to his captors when they entered his cell, or a beating would follow. When he was finally released in 1973, he had scars all over his body, boils from a skin infection that would never go away, teeth that fell out, and nerve damage in his arms and hands from the ropes and iron stocks. He passed away in 2006.

A few years ago, my sisters and I stood in for our dad at the United States Air Force Academy, at the unveiling of the Vietnam Memorial Pavilion, a tribute to the American prisoners of war. A six-foot-tall bronze sculpture stands at the entrance, depicting a prisoner of Vietnam with a gag in his mouth, and his hands bound tightly behind his back. The sculptor was charged with depicting the American soldier's insubordinate spirit in the face of abject humiliation. If you look very closely at the prisoner's bound hand, his middle finger is sticking up in defiance.

That must be where I learned it. The inner strength that arose in me that day on the bus might have come from my fighter pilot dad, who taught his daughters well. Never capitulate to a bully. It only strengthens and empowers the bully. And never make an alliance with a bully just to get something you want. The mean-spiritedness that fuels them is likely to rub off.

Do not be misled: "Bad company corrupts good character."[21]

---

21. 1 Cor 15:33 NIV.

5

Everything Is Uncovered

> You know why I do it? I do it to discredit you all and demean you all, so when you write negative stories about me, no one will believe you.—Donald Trump[1]

In 2002, a story broke in *The Boston Globe*, diligently researched for years by a small group of reporters, that had serious implications for millions of people around the world. It was about how the US Catholic Church covered up child molestation by simply shuttling offending priests from parish to parish. For decades, the sexual abuse was kept under wraps at every level. The traumatized children were told to be quiet. The shocked parents were urged by the Catholic Church to forget about it and move on. Bishops and other higher-ups felt the consequences for the abuse should stay within the church, and not be prosecuted legally, because they saw it as a sin for which priests could repent rather than an evil compulsion for which they should be put behind bars. And, of course, they didn't want the negative publicity.

The victimized families were too frightened to speak out, partly because they considered the priests and bishops to be authority figures who were put into position by God himself. The Catholic Church used Scriptures like this one to convince them that God wanted them to be quiet about the

---

1. Donald Trump to Lesley Stahl on why he attacks the media. Lesley Stahl, "Trump Admitted Mission to 'Discredit' Press," CBS, May 23, 2018, para. 4, https://www.cbsnews.com/news/lesley-stahl-donald-trump-said-attacking-press-to-discredit-negative-stories/.

abuse: "Let every person be subject to the governing authorities. For there is no authority except by God's appointment, and the authorities that exist have been instituted by God. So the person who resists such authority resists the ordinance of God, and those who resist will incur judgment."[2]

So now we are forced to add "spiritual abuse" to the list of atrocities already suffered by the victims and their families. Spiritual abuse is "a form of emotional and psychological abuse characterized by a systemic pattern of coercive and controlling behavior in a religious context. Spiritual abuse can have a deeply damaging impact on those who experience it. However, holding a theological position is not in itself inherently spiritually abusive, but misuse of Scripture, applied theology and doctrine is often a component of spiritually abusive behaviour."[3] God never intends verses about authority figures to excuse abusive, immoral behavior, or to keep people quiet. Scripture applied wrongly can be used to cover up any manner of evil.

More recently, in February 2019, the *Houston Chronicle* and the *San Antonio Express-News* exposed a history of sexual abuse within the Southern Baptist Convention.[4] Over seven hundred brave victims testified to devastating abuse and subsequent attempted cover-ups by the SBC. As if they had not already suffered enough, the victims were oftentimes met with opposition from leaders in the SBC who thought it best, "for the sake of Christianity," to protect the institution and the authority figures within it. The SBC's attempt to keep people quiet also constitutes spiritual abuse.

"For Everyone Who Does Evil Deeds Hates the Light and Does Not Come to the Light, So That Their Deeds Will Not Be Exposed"[5]

One role of a follower of Jesus is to shine a light on darkness and bring what is hidden out into the light. Jesus came to destroy the works of the

---

2. Rom 13:1–2 NET.

3. CCPAS, *Spiritual Abuse: A Position Paper* (Swanley, Eng.: CCPAS, 2018), 6, https://thirtyoneeight.org/media/4upcux21/spiritual-abuse-position-statement.pdf.

4. Kate Shellnut, "After Major Investigation, Southern Baptists Confront the Abuse Crisis They Knew Was Coming," *Christianity Today*, February 11, 2019, https://www.christianitytoday.com/news/2019/february/southern-baptist-abuse-investigation-houston-chronicle-sbc.html.

5. John 3:20 NET.

devil,[6] and we are called to follow suit, but we cannot expose what we refuse to acknowledge or what we are afraid to call out just because a person is an authority figure. Evil is evil. Just because someone is in a position of leadership does not mean they are above scrutiny—in fact, their behavior should be more closely examined.

Over the course of his presidency, Donald Trump made (and tweeted) hundreds, if not thousands, of rude, dishonest, demeaning, sexist, and racist remarks. And yet, under the guise of "remaining subject" to those in authority, many evangelical leaders chose to cover up for him. Some even claimed that Christians who were alarmed and offended by Trump's words should never criticize or correct him. This was classic spiritual abuse designed to keep people quiet, not unlike what the Catholic Church, and some leaders in the Southern Baptist Convention, employed against victimized families. Evangelical leaders who refused to denounce Trump's remarks were being used by the enemy to intimidate people from speaking out, and also to enable his cruelty.

Bullying is evil. Mocking people is evil. White nationalism is evil. Sexual assault, and the glossing over of it, is evil. God is not glorified when abuse and/or bad decisions are covered up by pulling the "governing authority" card. No leader—political, religious, academic, business, or otherwise—is above scrutiny and correction. Ever. If you think something is wrong, speak up and don't let anyone intimidate you into staying silent. Eugene Peterson puts it this way in his translation of John 3:19–21:

> This is the crisis we're in: God-light streamed into the world, but men and women everywhere ran for the darkness. They went for the darkness because they were not really interested in pleasing God. Everyone who makes a practice of doing evil, addicted to denial and illusion, hates God-light and won't come near it, fearing a painful exposure. But anyone working and living in truth and reality welcomes God-light so the work can be seen for the God-work it is.[7]

With that, the free press is absolutely critical to our democracy. Any war on it only shows that the person warring has something to hide. Investigative journalism is detective work. It was the dogged determination of investigative journalists that uncovered Watergate, exposed the child molestation in the Catholic Church, exposed the sexual abuse cover-ups

---

6. 1 John 3:8b.
7. John 3:19–21.

in the Southern Baptist Convention, assisted in dismantling the abusive leadership at Mars Hill Church, revealed the dangers of Scientology and other cults so that victims could be free, and finally brought the Harvey Weinstein and Larry Nassar sexual assault allegations out into the open.

* * *

In the last decade, Evangelicalism has suffered the downfall of one prominent leader after another. Thanks to the courageous victims who came forward to tell their stories, and to solid and credible reporting, Jerry Falwell Jr., Ravi Zacharias, Bill Gothard, and Jean Vanier have been exposed as sexual predators. Many others touted as "celebrities" within Evangelicalism have seen their ministries injured by extramarital affairs. (I use the term "extramarital affair" generously. A more accurate phrasing may be "preyed on women in their churches, over whom they possessed a convenient spiritual authority.") In any case, despite their fruitful ministries, God saw fit to bring out into the light what they preferred to hide. These are all cases involving leaders in positions of authority, and they are all cases in which the Scriptures about governing authorities do not overrule God's mandate that lies and abuse must be uncovered and brought into the light. God doesn't *need* a Liberty University, a Hillsong, or a Willow Creek. He can start a new, even more fruitful ministry anywhere, anytime. What he wants, rather, what he insists on, is that his sheep are safely shepherded. Hear this now, church leaders: you can have a ministry seemingly exploding with fruitfulness, expanding north, south, east, and west, abundant in baptisms and rich in good deeds, but if just one person within your ministry is being hurt or exploited, God will eventually shine a spotlight to guide his sheep out of hidden darkness, even if it topples your entire ministry.

In the same way, God doesn't *need* a Trump for Christianity to prosper in America. And this may come as a shock to white American Evangelicals who have been conditioned to believe otherwise, but he also doesn't *need* a United States of America. We are no more or less special to him than any other country on planet Earth.[8] Love of country is wonderful, but idolatry of country is quite a different matter. America could dissolve tomorrow, and the kingdom of God would be unconcerned. The gospel does not begin and end on American soil. It originates in heaven, and when God has a

---

8. "For there is no partiality with God" (Rom 2:11 NET).

mind to bring his kingdom to earth, he can use any people he wills, any nation he wills, any time, any old way he chooses.

* * *

"Rip the Cover Off Those Frauds and See How Attractive They Look in the Light of Christ" [9]

It's a dangerous man with much to hide who will go to great lengths to avoid exposure. Journalist Katy Tur was assigned to cover Trump's first campaign, and followed him closely for five hundred days. Where Trump went, Katy and her camera team went. Like he did with Megyn Kelly, Trump first tried to butter her up for positive coverage. But Katy remained true to the facts, and he quickly became furious when she called out his falsehoods. When he exaggerated the size of his crowds to the media, she stepped in to correct him.[10] When he said he was self-financing his campaign, she reminded him that he was spending much more of the donors' money than his own.[11] When he brought out steaks wrapped in plastic that said "Trump," Katy pointed out the fine print—they were from another company, his staff had put fake labels on them. Trump Steaks had actually been pulled from the shelves in 2007.[12] When he got booed at a summit in Washington, DC, Katy asked him to respond on camera. "I didn't get boos," Trump lied, with the camera pointed right at his face. "I got cheers." He went on to tell her that the boos were actually for her.[13] Resigned that he couldn't charm her or stop her coverage of him, he tried another method of gaining power over her—he grabbed and kissed her in the hallway of a news station.[14] While she stood frozen in the hallway, offended and embarrassed in front of her crew, he went on *Morning Joe* and bragged that he had just kissed her, as if they were the best friends in the world.[15] Katy, mortified but undeterred, continued to do her job. In exchange for her accurate reporting, he berated

9. Eph 5:11.
10. Tur, *Unbelievable*, 50.
11. Tur, *Unbelievable*, 50–51.
12. Tur, *Unbelievable*, 152–53.
13. Tur, *Unbelievable*, 51.
14. Tur, *Unbelievable*, 54.
15. Tur, *Unbelievable*, 55–56.

her on TV and on Twitter, calling her "awful," "terrible," "third-rate," "dishonest," "incompetent," and "the worst." He singled her out at his rallies, belittled her and slung abuse, referring to her as "Little Katy." The crowd turned and glared at her. They called her ugly and a "dumb c#^t." His supporters became so inflamed against her, the Secret Service had to walk her to her car to ensure she wasn't attacked. Insults and terror poured into her phone. Trump followers accused her of sleeping her way to the top. They threatened to kill her.[16] But that wasn't even the worst.

At one of his rallies, Trump inexplicably veered off of his speech to let everyone know what a great job Vladimir Putin was doing on rebuilding Russia and its image. Never mind that Putin has his political opponents murdered, invades countries, launches cyberattacks on other nations, and has homosexual people beaten and thrown in jail. Donald Trump was holding him up as someone to be admired. Then he casually slipped in, "You know, he's killed reporters."[17] His followers went into overdrive. Six thousand Trump supporters turned in unison and began booing against the thirty or so journalists who were confined together in the press pen in the center of the arena. Trump antagonized them even more, pointing to the photographers in the front and saying they'd been let out of their "cage." "I hate them. I'd never kill them, but I do hate them. Some of them are such lying, disgusting people."[18] Trump knows full well how his more manic followers respond to him. Bringing up an authoritarian world leader who has reporters killed was not a joke. It was not a mistake. It was a threat.

Posting a picture of an angry mob screaming at and hurling abuse while flipping off reporters, journalist Jim Acosta expressed concern: "Just a sample of the sad scene we faced at the Trump rally in Tampa. I'm very worried that the hostility whipped up by Trump and some conservative media will result in somebody getting hurt. We should not treat our fellow Americans this way. The press is not the enemy."[19]

"Believe me, if I become president, oh, do they have problems," Trump said, referring to the media as "the opposition party." "They're going to have such problems."[20] And it was true. Journalists critical of

---

16. Tur, *Unbelievable*, 50–51, 68, 174.
17. Tur, *Unbelievable*, 97.
18. Tur, *Unbelievable*, 99.
19. Jim Acosta (@Acosta), "Just a sample of the sad scene," Twitter, August 1, 2018, 6:32 p.m., https://twitter.com/Acosta/status/1024467940257738752.
20. Callum Borchers, "As Trump Calls the Media 'the Opposition Party,' Here

Trump had reason to fear for their safety. He created an atmosphere in which it became permissible to hurt them, and he continued to fan the flames of violence until his bitter end. As a direct result of Trump's antagonism, reporters endured violent online abuse and some, including David Fahrenthold, Megyn Kelly, Jared Yates Sexton, Katy Tur, and Eboni K. Williams, had their lives threatened. But he never apologized for frenetic followers acting on behalf of their leader, and he did nothing to quell the abuse. Instead, he went out of his way to provoke it. He repeatedly referred to the media as the "Enemy of the People." He tweeted a video of himself punching an image of a CNN reporter in the head,[21] which got his fanatical supporters agitated again. A pipe bomb delivery, and a bomb threat to CNN's New York offices, ensued.[22]

Scripture instructs, "Have nothing to do with the fruitless deeds of darkness, but rather expose them."[23] In the end, Trump's strategy of threatening reporters didn't work. The truth came out, and it continues to unravel around him. That's because God is the ultimate truth teller, and uncovering darkness is the Lord's work. Those who try to silence people who bring darkness into the light will be called to account, and that includes leaders in the evangelical church who aimed to convince people that they should ignore or falsify Trump's misdeeds. "Nothing in all creation is hidden from God's sight. Everything is uncovered and laid bare before the eyes of him to whom we must give account."[24]

Rest assured, God will eventually expose all predators, abusers, liars, con men, and bullies. And he may just use a reporter to do it.

Are 4 Threats to Press Freedom," *Washington Post*, January 27, 2016, para. 3, https://www.washingtonpost.com/news/the-fix/wp/2016/11/10/4-threats-to-the-media-under-president-trump/.

21. Daniella Silva, "President Trump Tweets Wrestling Video of Himself Attacking 'CNN,'" NBC, July 2, 2017, https://www.nbcnews.com/politics/donald-trump/president-trump-tweets-wwe-video-himself-attacking-cnn-n779031.

22. Chris Baynes, "CNN Offices Evacuated in Bomb Scare Just as Trump Tweeted, 'ENEMY OF THE PEOPLE' about Media He Doesn't Like," *Independent*, December 7, 2018, https://www.independent.co.uk/news/world/americas/cnn-bomb-threat-offices-evacuated-new-york-trump-tweet-enenmy-people-fake-news-a8672356.html.

23. Eph 5:11 NIV.

24. Heb 4:13 NIV.

6

The Fox

[Jesus] replied, "Go tell that fox, 'I will keep on driving out demons and healing people today and tomorrow, and on the third day I will reach my goal.'"—Luke 13:32 NIV

Once upon a time there lived a vain ruler, Herod Antipas, the son of Herod the Great. He was the ruler of Galilee, a region in Northern Israel where Jesus often ministered. Having inherited a great amount of wealth from his father, Herod Antipas was notably self-centered and loved to flaunt his money. Building gold-plated, lavish fortresses for himself was his favorite pastime.

King Herod was not inwardly virtuous, but he was crafty enough to realize that having the favor of the Jewish people was to his benefit. When it suited him, he put on their religion like a cloak. It was to his political advantage to participate in their feasts and rituals, and to sit piously as the recipient of their prayers. Most of them went along with his ruse, although one Jewish man in particular did not. John the Baptist considered Herod to be an unfit ruler and an unscrupulous adulterer. And he wasn't afraid to say so.

It went like this: when his wife got too old, King Herod divorced her for a younger woman, who happened to be his brother's much younger wife—who also happened to be his niece by another brother. Even for those days, it was a scandalous union. John the Baptist's criticism of the relationship angered Herod, but Herod kept himself under control until one fateful night, when his impulsivity and lack of moral fiber got the best of him. He was so overtaken by his wife's young daughter, who was dancing for him, that he offered her whatever she wanted. Having already been coached by her mother, the girl knew what to ask for. John had rebuked him for his immorality, and *wham!*, Herod ordered his head on a platter.

Jesus and Herod

Jesus took some time alone to mourn his cousin's gruesome death, and then he got back to work. He went throughout Galilee teaching the love of God, healing people, feeding the hungry, and generally antagonizing the ultra-religious. They tried to run him out of town, figuring that after the untimely death of his cousin, there would be no one better to scare him off than their own unstable king, Herod Antipas. So they invoked his name in an effort to intimidate Jesus:

> At that time some Pharisees came to Jesus and said to him, "Leave this place and go somewhere else. Herod wants to kill you."[1]

But Jesus was not frightened by Herod, and refused to yield to their demand. In fact, he insulted the political ruler of his day:

> Go tell that fox, "I will keep on driving out demons and healing people today and tomorrow, and on the third day I will reach my goal."[2]

It's not surprising that Jesus used that word. Jesus looked right inside Herod's unrepentant heart and pulled out the truth, as Jesus was prone to do. A fox is a wily, reckless, and, according to Israelite holiness codes, ritually unclean animal. Hidden under the guise of "zeal for the law" and religious customs, was a morally depraved, impetuous, cunning ruler, and Jesus was not about to bow down or provide religious cover for him. Like his cousin before him, Jesus knew that telling the truth was more honoring to God than promoting a lie, even if the lie seemed to benefit their religion.

I wonder if Jesus would use the same word to describe our former president. Donald Trump spent his entire life building a lavish empire to himself. Prior to the presidency, he had never volunteered even a day of service toward the common good. He certainly never put himself in the

---

1. Luke 13:31 NIV.
2. Luke 13:32 NIV.

way of military service, although he had the audacity to insult people who have. And his "donations" to charity have been found to be fraudulent on more than one occasion.[3] He sought only to make his own name great with Trump Tower, Trump Taj Mahal, Trump Plaza, Trump Castle, Trump Jets, Trump Steaks, Trump Vodka, Trump Model Management, Trump Productions, Trump Wine, Trump Water, Trump Mortgages, Trump Golf Courses, Trump Cologne, and Trump University, until there was only one thing left to put his name on: Trump's United States of America.

Trump's only motivation in life is to enlarge himself, and he uses whomever suits his needs at the time. When it boosted his image to discuss threesomes on the radio with Howard Stern, he went on air and discussed threesomes with Howard Stern. But when it benefited him to change his image and start hanging out with religious folk, which would garner him evangelical votes, that's exactly what he did. He suddenly became a born-again Christian, offering conservatives everything they ever wanted, and then some. Trump is a chameleon, playing whatever role will keep him on top. And many in the church played along.

Herod Antipas was not the first leader to exploit religious people, and he won't be the last. There will always be men who take up religion in order to elevate themselves. The evangelical church would do well, moving forward, to identify this type of political manipulation early on and steer clear of it. The apostle Paul issues the following warnings about exploitative leaders:

> They'll make a show of religion. . . . Unscrupulous conmen will continue to exploit the faith. They're as deceived as the people they lead astray. As long as they are out there, things can only get worse.[4]

> Tag them for what they are: ignorant windbags who infect the air with germs of envy, controversy, bad-mouthing, suspicious rumors. Eventually there's an epidemic of backstabbing, and truth is but a distant memory. They think religion is a way to make a fast buck.[5]

---

3. "Donald J. Trump Pays Court-Ordered $2 Million for Illegally Using Trump Foundation Funds," New York State Attorney General, December 10, 2019, https://ag.ny.gov/press-release/2019/donald-j-trump-pays-court-ordered-2-million-illegally-using-trump-foundation.

4. 2 Tim 3:5, 13.

5. 1 Tim 6:2–5.

A Jesus-following church will rise up against such a leader, not acquiesce just to see what it can get out of him.

Upon the advice of his religious council, Trump attempted to tone down his divisive rhetoric mid-presidency, but, like Herod, his impulsive nature ruled him. He openly mocked political opponents, insulted reporters, and promoted violence toward those who dared criticize or vote against him up until the bitter end. There was never the slightest hint of repentance toward anyone he publicly maligned, nor to those who have gone to prison for committing violence on his behalf. In the absence of his repentance and any detectable fruit of the spirit, for the church to even remotely suggest that Donald Trump follows Jesus, or is operating on his behalf, is a complete mockery of the God we serve. God will not be mocked.

Why would Jesus be any more okay with Trump's charade than he was with Herod's? More than likely, ongoing evangelical support of Donald Trump has tried his patience.

> You have wearied the Lord with your words.
> "How have we wearied him?" you ask.
> By saying, "All who do evil are good in the eyes of the Lord, and he is pleased with them."[6]

Inciting violence toward the free press so that they have to hire bodyguards? God is not pleased. Cussing out NFL players for shedding light on police brutality? God is not pleased. Abusing his own staff and insulting members of Congress and degrading the FBI in an attempt to hide his crimes? God is not pleased. Equating Nazis with Nazi protesters at Charlottesville? God is not pleased. Constantly berating women's forms and faces? God is not pleased. Insulting mayors and governors who are just trying to keep their citizens alive? God is not pleased. Mocking people with physical disabilities? God is not pleased. *Any form of abuse is unacceptable to God. Period.* We have a right to hold our president accountable. More than that, we have a responsibility. The world should not have to wonder if God is okay with Trump's violent rhetoric and ill treatment of people. Anything less than a swift and hearty rebuke from the evangelical church is an inaccurate, gross misrepresentation of the Lord we serve. John the Baptist wouldn't stand for this mockery of what God will, and absolutely will not, put up with. His headless body is probably rolling over in his tomb right now.

6. Mal 2:17 NIV.

For all of his trying to win favor with the Jews, and follow their customs when it suited him, one thing is clear from the Scriptures: Herod Antipas was not really interested in following God. And his pandering to religious folk couldn't fool Christ. Covering his misbehavior with religious fervor may have been enough to pacify some religious leaders, but it sure didn't work on the Lord. Jesus doesn't play along. Jesus doesn't lie, and Jesus doesn't pretend.

Go tell that fox: Jesus sees right through his facade.

7

Spritzing for Jesus

> Everywhere we go, people breathe in the exquisite fragrance. Because of Christ, we give off a sweet scent rising to God, which is recognized by those on the way of salvation—an aroma redolent with life.—2 Cor 2:14–16

It's weird when you see "the world" acting more Christlike than the church. Such was the case, at least on my social media feeds, during COVID. Some in the church balked and complained, and even flat-out refused to wear masks or comply with their city- and state-sanctioned safety measures, which were designed to protect susceptible people and ultimately benefit the common good. One Christian told me that she was perfectly healthy, why should she be inconvenienced at the grocery store by wearing a mask? If elderly or immunocompromised people needed to shop for groceries, they could order them online. "Amazon delivers," she said. It didn't sound very neighborly, let alone like someone willing to lay down her own life in service to "the least of these."[1] It was one of those times that made me wonder if some Evangelicals were following the spirit of Jesus, who, according to the Gospels, cared about people's health, or the spirit of Trump. The spirit of Trump, as discussed in the preface of this book, is characterized by narcissism, callousness, and bullying.

The pandemic seemed to bring out the worst of the Trumpian attributes. My brother Kevin, who at the time was the general manager

---

1. Matt 25:40.

of a Costco near Atlanta, Georgia, became overwhelmed with having to protect his employees against belligerent customers, many of whom professed themselves to be Christ followers. I felt compelled to apologize to him on their behalf. I couldn't help but contrast such selfish obstinance with the graciousness of the apostle Paul, who said, "Do nothing out of selfish ambition or vain conceit. Rather, in humility value others above yourselves, not looking to your own interests but each of you to the interests of the others."[2] (Phil 2:3–4 NIV).

* * *

During our state's COVID quarantine in March 2020, someone left the cabinet door open under our kitchen sink, and our little Yorkie, Vivi, helped herself to the contents of the compost bucket. She had a heyday before we caught her, looking up guiltily at us with the string from a roast chicken hanging out of her mouth. She'd had enough time to work her way through a hardy array of chicken bones, eggshells, and coffee grounds, and the result was an ungodly amount of diarrhea for days. You'd be astonished at the output a tiny seven-pound ball of fluff can make. We walked down to Walgreens and bought some infant diapers for her, hoping to contain some of the mess. It turns out that baby diapers don't actually work well on a dog, even after Steve cut a hole for her tail. On day three, with no end in sight, I finally quarantined Vivi to a room of her own.

I gave her a fresh diaper and set her up on a paper mat in our bedroom (no rugs or carpet in there!) with Squeak-ums, her squeaky hedgehog, and closed the door. After about an hour, I went to peek in on her. She was sheepish. She had wiggled out of her diaper and made a mess by the French doors. I'm embarrassed to say that I didn't have it in me to clean more Vivi poo, so I left it. I figured it was Steve's turn—he could clean it up after his conference call. I sprayed some of Mrs. Meyer's rose-scented room spray to try to cover up the smell, shut the door, and went about my business. It turned out Steve had back-to-back Zoom meetings, so I just kept opening the door, spritzing some rose spray, and shutting the door again.

Untended poo, fuming in the corner of a room full of rose-scented cover-up, is what the spirit of Trumpism smells like in the church. During the pandemic, the overwhelming hypocrisy of the "pro-life" crowd hit its peak. Somehow, shouts of *"But my personal rights!"* overrode care and concern for other peoples' lives and health. In a scary time when the

2. Phil 2:3–4 NIV.

world most needed to see Christ's humility, love, and compassion toward them, the "me-first" attitude of some in the church was hugely noticeable to those outside of it. My sister Jane asked me, "Isn't the church supposed to care about sick people?" "Yes, when they're following Jesus," I replied. "Just not when they're following Fox News."

It was useless to try to explain Trumpism hypocrisy to my family, which, by 2020, had reached a whole new level of absurdity. They had already watched in horrified wonderment as we—the evangelical church—championed Focus on the Family but somehow defended traumatizing little children by separating them from their parents at the border. They watched as we—the church (who had loudly condemned the sexual ethics of Bill Clinton, saying his behavior made him unfit for the presidency)—condemned the sexual ethics of the LBGTQ community at the same time as we winked at the escapades of a man who had had an affair with a porn star while his wife was home tending their infant son. My brother and sisters watched as the church tooted its own horn to the same self-righteous note we always hide behind—"We are pro-life!"—even as we snickered at mask wearing and stronger common-sense gun laws, two tangible things that also save lives. Steve and I were speechless. Through our family's eyes, we saw what the world saw: over the Trump years, the church enabled, defended, and justified immorality to such a degree that we became a parody of ourselves, and we didn't even know it.

Trump paid hush money in an attempt to cover up his affairs with a porn star and a Playboy Bunny six days before the 2016 election; we looked the other way. He refused to turn over his "big, beautiful" tax returns; we decided transparency wasn't important after all. He told lie after easily provable lie; we joined him in blaming the media. Trump bullied a female reporter; we said she asked for it when she took the job. Trump shut the door on refugees in danger, in direct contradiction to our Savior's instructions; we said he was keeping us safe. Trump made fun of a physically handicapped person; we denied it as the world saw the evidence on video and recoiled in disgust. Trump called Nazis "good people" and forwarded a white supremacist's tweet; we called it a slip of the tongue and an unfortunate mis-tweet. On every occasion, the church just spritzed a little more rose-scented air freshener into the air in hopes it would distract from Trump's toxic fumes. Lie, lie, justify, justify, enable, enable. Spritz, spritz, spritz. After all, in the midst of all the lies and corruption, we still believed we stood for the right things. We told ourselves we were spritzing for Jesus.

But the world could smell the dog poop a mile away.

8

An Open Door for the Devil

> But what comes out of the mouth proceeds from the heart, and this defiles a man.—Matt 15:18 RSV

If you've spent any time at all in the evangelical church, you know it is big on sexual morality. I was surprised, actually, coming into the church as a married woman in my twenties, at how much time at the pulpit was given to sexual purity. The gospel of purity was taught so much, I was given to understand it was akin to the gospel of salvation. The church's teaching on immorality taught me that when we look at or participate in any sexual activity outside of marriage between a man and a woman, our minds and our bodies can become defiled. In regard to a connection with immorality, Paul writes, "Therefore, since we have these promises, dear friends, let us cleanse ourselves from everything that could defile the body and the spirit, and thus accomplish holiness out of reverence for God" (2 Cor 7:1 NIV). A quote by a famous pastor sticks with me to this day: "What entertains you . . . enters you." I believed the church's teaching that to choose a lifestyle steeped in sexual immorality was to leave an open door for the devil.

Donald Trump added to his Atlantic City casino in 2013, turning thirty-six thousand square feet of it into a strip club featuring women in G-strings and pasties, and "modified" lap dancing.[1] He had a cameo in a

---

1. Seth Augenstein, "Nation's First Casino Strip Club Coming to Atlantic City," NJ, July 4, 2013, https://www.nj.com/atlantic/2013/07/strip_club_coming_to_atlantic_city_casino_reports_say.html.

"soft core" pornographic movie. He was a frequent guest on the Howard Stern show, making crude and degrading comments about women. The men discussed watching Paris Hilton's sex tape, having sex with women on their menstrual cycles, threesomes, whether or not they would sleep with certain celebrities, and dumping women aged over thirty-five.[2] Trump announced that a flat-chested woman was "very hard to be a ten."[3] He bragged about walking unannounced through a room full of naked beauty contestants because he was the pageant's owner and could "get away with things like that."[4] (Pageant contestants have said that they were made to come out one by one and parade in front of him so that he could rate them. Miss Washington 2013 Cassandra Searles wrote that Trump "treated us like cattle" during her pageant experience.)[5]

To date, twenty-six women accuse Trump of sexual assault. They all have similar stories—that he kissed them or shoved his tongue down their throat and grabbed their genitals without consent.[6] And just so there would be no confusion as to whether these assaults occurred, God made sure the *Access Hollywood* tape was released prior to the 2016 election. This made it possible for Evangelicals to actually hear Donald Trump confessing to the criminal sexual assault he had already been accused of.

> You know I'm automatically attracted to beautiful. . . . I just start kissing them. It's like a magnet. Just kiss. I don't even wait. And when you're a star they let you do it. You can do anything. Grab 'em by the p*ssy. You can do anything.[7]

---

2. Rena Flores, "More Crude Donald Trump Tapes Surface from the Howard Stern Show," CBS, October 9, 2016, https://www.cbsnews.com/news/more-donald-trump-tapes-surface-from-howard-stern-show/.

3. Alan Rappeport, "Donald Trump's Trail of Comments about Women," *New York Times*, March 25, 2016, https://www.nytimes.com/2016/03/26/us/politics/donald-trump-women.html.

4. Flores, "More Crude Donald Trump Tapes," para. 7.

5. Levi Pulkkinen, "Former Miss Washington among Trump's Accusers," *SeattlePI*, October 12, 2016, para. 4, https://www.seattlepi.com/seattlenews/article/Former-Miss-Washington-among-Trump-s-accusers-9967858.php.

6. Eliza Relman and Azmi Haroun, "The 26 Women Who Have Accused Trump of Sexual Misconduct," *Business Insider*, September 17, 2020, https://www.businessinsider.com/women-accused-trump-sexual-misconduct-list-2017-12.

7. Mark Makela, "Transcript: Donald Trump's Taped Comments about Women," *New York Times*, October 8, 2016, https://www.nytimes.com/2016/10/08/us/donald-trump-tape-transcript.html.

Anytime a man views a woman as an opportunity for sexual advance and acts on that opportunity without her consent, he is defiled by, and in cooperation with, the enemy. And yet, even after having his criminal behavior confirmed by his own words, some Evangelicals refused to rescind support. In her 2023 memoir, evangelist and Bible study teacher Beth Moore reflects on the pain she felt as male church leaders rationalized Trump's comments. "It was just locker room talk. He's a baby Christian. He's not the same man. He made mistakes. He was just big talking like men do sometimes. Boys will be boys. . . . A few voiced disgust, and I was grateful for those, but most either remained silent or actually offered excuses. My own brothers in the faith, who'd been easily scandalized by others, had developed a sudden and protracted case of uncharacteristic tolerance."[8]

This "sudden and protracted case of uncharacteristic tolerance" Mrs. Moore describes is in keeping with the attitude of Judas, which downplays criminality and misogyny as long as it gets power.

Donald Trump not only treats women as objects that he can grab when the urge strikes him, but he has a history of sexualizing young girls, including his own daughters. He referred to Ivanka as very voluptuous, remarking that if she weren't his daughter he would perhaps be dating her. He told Howard Stern that it was acceptable to call her a "piece of ass," and said she was "hot."

> You know who's one of the great beauties of the world—according to everybody—and I created her? Ivanka. My daughter, Ivanka. She's six feet tall, she's got the best body.
>
> If I weren't happily married, and ya know, her father . . .[9]

When his daughter Tiffany was an infant, Trump said, "She's a really beautiful baby, and she's got Marla's legs." Motioning to his chest, he went on to add, "We don't know whether she's got this part yet, but time will tell."[10] When he met Paris Hilton for the first time, at age twelve, she walked into the room with her parents and he asked, "Who the hell is that?"[11]

---

8. Beth Moore, *All My Knotted Up Life: A Memoir* (Carol Stream, IL: Tyndale, 2023), 240.

9. Associated Press, "Trump Jokes That He'd Date Daughter," *Today*, March 7, 2006, para. 4, https://www.today.com/popculture/trump-jokes-he-d-date-daughter-wbna11714379.

10. Meg Wagner, "See It: Donald Trump Comments on 1-Year-Old Daughter's Breasts in Disturbing 1994 Interview," *New York Daily News*, April 7, 2016, para. 5, https://www.nydailynews.com/news/politics/trump-comments-1-year-old-daughter-breasts-article-1.2591961.

11. Alana Horowitz Satlin, "Trump Admits He Found 12-Year-Old Paris Hilton

Referring to Lindsay Lohan, who was eighteen years old at the time, he said,

> I've seen a, you know, close up of her chest and a lot of freckles.... She's probably deeply troubled, and therefore great in bed. How come the deeply troubled women, you know, deeply, deeply troubled, they're always the best in bed?[12]

A news camera caught him as he approached a ten-year-old girl, asked her if she was going to be riding up the escalator, and then made a comment that he would be dating her someday.[13] Another camera caught him as he sidled up to a group of young girls singing Christmas carols with a youth choir outside Manhattan's Plaza Hotel. Trump asked two of them how old they were. When they said they were fourteen, he replied, "Wow! Just think—in a couple of years I'll be dating you."[14]

There have been three rape allegations to date. One by Ivana Trump in a sworn deposition, which she retracted later when it came time to negotiate the financials of their divorce settlement.[15] Another by a woman who filed a federal lawsuit in 2016, but withdrew it when she received death threats.[16] And a third by reporter E. Jean Carroll, to whom a jury awarded $5 million in damages after finding Trump liable for sexual assault and defamation.[17] Unfortunately, the verdict didn't stop him from

---

Attractive," *HuffPost*, September 30, 2016, https://www.huffpost.com/entry/trump-paris-hilton_n_57ee9373e4b024a52d2ea629.

12. Andrew Kaczynski and Nathan McDermott, "Trump on Lindsay Lohan in 2004: 'Deeply Troubled' Women Are 'Always the Best in Bed,'" CNN, October 14, 2016, paras. 9, 16, https://money.cnn.com/2016/10/14/media/donald-trump-on-lindsay-lohan/.

13. German Lopez, "Donald Trump Once Saw a Child on an Escalator and Said, "I'm Going to Be Dating Her in 10 Years,'" *Vox*, October 12, 2016, https://www.vox.com/policy-and-politics/2016/10/12/13265670/trump-10-year-old-girl.

14. Seema Mehta, "Donald Trump Once Told 14-Year-Old Girls, 'In a Couple of Years, I'll Be Dating You,'" *Los Angeles Times*, October 13, 2016, para. 2, https://www.latimes.com/nation/politics/trailguide/la-na-trailguide-updates-20161013-htmlstory.html#donald-trump-once-told-14-year-old-girls-in-a-couple-of-years-ill-be-dating-you.

15. Relman, "26 Women Who Have Accused."

16. Rory Carroll, "Woman Accusing Trump of Raping Her at 13 Cancels Her Plan to Go Public," *Guardian*, November 3, 2016, https://www.theguardian.com/us-news/2016/nov/02/donald-trump-rape-lawsuit-13-year-old-cancels-public-event.

17. Adam Reiss and Dareh Gregorian, "Trump Found Liable for Sexually Abusing and Defaming E. Jean Carroll in Civil Trial and Is Ordered to Pay $5 Million," NBC, May 9, 2023, https://www.nbcnews.com/politics/donald-trump/jury-reaches-verdict-e-jean-carroll-rape-defamation-case-trump-rcna82778.

AN OPEN DOOR FOR THE DEVIL

bullying her. Less than a year later, he was ordered to pay Carroll an additional $83.3 million, by a separate jury, for his ongoing defamation and social media attacks against her.[18]

While married to Melania, Donald had at least two affairs, with an adult film actress and with a Playboy Bunny, and paid them hush money right before the 2016 election in a (futile) effort to keep them from talking.[19] I don't think it's a stretch to conclude that, somewhere along the way, according to the evangelical church's own teaching, Donald Trump left "an open door for the devil."

If only there was a way we could know for sure. If only Jesus gave us some clue as to how we might determine if someone had been defiled by lust, abuse, and misogyny. Oh, wait. He did.

> A good man brings good things out of the good stored up in his heart, and an evil man brings evil things out of the evil stored up in his heart. For the mouth speaks what the heart is full of.[20]

So what was in Trump's heart when he was calling women "fat," "pig," "dog," "slob," "bimbo," "disgusting animal," and saying of women, "You have to treat them like s---"?[21] What had a hold of his heart when he publicly shamed a beauty contestant for gaining weight, calling her "Miss Piggy"? Or when he told a contestant on *The Apprentice* that she must have made a pretty picture dropping to her knees? Or when he told a *New York Times* columnist, "You have the face of a dog?"[22] As recently as 2020, he called women "nasty," "monster," and "crazed lunatic."

The same evangelical church that taught me biblical truths on immorality discarded their own teaching when it became politically convenient for them to do so. But women with spiritually attuned ears know

---

18. Larry Neumeister et al., "Donald Trump Must Pay an Additional $83.3 Million to E. Jean Carroll in Defamation Case, Jury Says," *AP*, January 24, 2024, https://apnews.com/article/trump-carroll-defamation-trial-e4ea8b93cdeb29857864ffd8d14be888.

19. Jonathan Allen and Jonathan Stempel, "FBI Documents Point to Trump Role in Hush Money for Porn Star Daniels," *Reuters*, July 18, 2019, https://www.reuters.com/article/us-usa-trump-cohen/fbi-documents-point-to-trump-role-in-hush-money-for-porn-star-daniels-idUSKCN1UD18D.

20. Luke 6:45 NIV.

21. Claire Cohen, "Donald Trump Sexism Tracker: Every Offensive Comment in One Place," *Telegraph*, November 7, 2020, http://www.telegraph.co.uk/women/politics/donald-trump-sexism-tracker-every-offensive-comment-in-one-place.

22. "28 Years of Donald Trump Insulting Women," Vox Media, n.d. https://apps.voxmedia.com/graphics/vox-trump-misogny-timeline/.

evil when they hear it. And women who have been sexually assaulted know evil when it grabs them.

> You know, it doesn't really matter what they write, as long as you've got a young and beautiful piece of ass.—Donald J. Trump[23]

---

23. Rappeport, "Donald Trump's Trail of Comments."

9

Test the Spirits

Dear friends, do not believe every spirit, but test the spirits to determine if they are from God, because many false prophets have gone out into the world.—1 John 4:1

Not every world leader is chosen by God. If they were, the Bible would not issue so many warnings about false leaders. Proverbs 25:5 says, "Remove the wicked from leadership and authority will be credible and God-honoring." The longer Donald Trump went on promoting conspiracy theories, calling for violence, and labeling anyone who criticized him "fake news," the more concerning it became that our fellow Evangelicals were backing him. Much of the church was besotted by his conservative promises, which desperately tumbled forth from his mouth in an attempt to cater to the religious right. Those bewitching promises were so bright and attractive, they blinded some Evangelicals from following standard biblical protocol for weighing a leader, which is to "test the spirits."[1]

Psychologists all over the world, including his own niece Dr. Mary Trump, sounded the alarm on the dangers of Trump's narcissistic personality disorder, but many professing Christ paid little heed. They wanted the power Trump could provide. Steve and I felt the sting of this betrayal. The church had taught us that character in leadership mattered greatly, that words carried weight, and that women should be treated with utmost

---

1. 1 John 4:1.

dignity and respect. Now they were doing a complete 180. I was worried for our country and also worried for the church who was willing to put their integrity on the line for a sociopath.

I decided to study leaders with sociopathic disorders. I was most interested in the warning signs and what it was about sociopaths that attracted people in such large numbers. I chose Dr. Robert G. L. Waite, professor of history at Williams College, and his book *The Psychopathic God: Adolf Hitler*, because Hitler was obviously the most dangerous sociopathic leader I could think of, and this was the most comprehensive literature I could find. I wanted to study his early life, his habits, mannerisms, and his complex and bizarre persona. There must have been warning signs, so what was it about him that made him electable? What were his promises to those who elected him?

Likewise, I wanted to engage in a deeper analysis of Trump's early life and his personality as experienced by friends and coworkers, in the most comprehensive biography possible. I wanted it to be a book in which he himself had engaged. I chose *Trump Revealed: An American Journey of Ambition, Ego, Money, and Power*, written by Michael Kranish, an award-winning investigative reporter, and Marc Fisher, an award-winning editor from *The Washington Post*. The *Post* employed a team of over twenty-five people to research, fact-check, and examine Donald Trump's childhood, habits, business deals, and the things that make him tick. Trump himself contributed over twenty hours of interviews and made his lawyer and some members of his campaign staff available. (He refused to let the authors talk to his siblings or to current and former Trump executives who have signed nondisclosure agreements. He also declined to give them access to his income tax returns.)[2] I also read *Too Much and Never Enough: How My Family Created the World's Most Dangerous Man* by Mary L. Trump, PhD, which gave additional insight into his early family life, relationship with his parents and siblings, mental instability, and the corrupt business practices he learned from his dad.

Hitler's murderous cruelty was inhumane, demonic, and without rival. I don't want to diminish it by comparing it to Trump. But as far as behavioral psychoanalysis goes, the similarities in their personalities are stunning. Numerous articles have been written on the likenesses between the two men. Peter Ross Range wrote, "To any serious student of Hitler's frightening and unforeseen rise to power in Germany, the recurring

---

2. Kranish and Fisher, *Trump Revealed*, 367.

echoes in Trump's speeches, interviews, and his underlying thinking have become too blatant to overlook."³

What follows are the shared personality traits between the two men, which are common among sociopaths and should, especially when taken all together, serve as warning signs.

Boastful Arrogance

One would be hard pressed to find a more boastful leader than Adolf Hitler, who talked about himself constantly and wanted to be perceived as strong and virile at all times. In one recorded incident when he felt competitive with his military commander, he suddenly stretched forth his hand in a Nazi salute, lowered his voice an octave and boomed:

> I can hold my arm like that for two solid hours. I never feel tired.... My arm is like granite—rigid and unbending. But Göring can't stand it. He has to drop his hand after half an hour in this salute. He's flabby. But I am hard.⁴

Hitler had a childlike temperament, with no capacity for mental or emotional growth. He often claimed that people were unfair and everyone was against him. He could not abide the thought of his own mistakes, would never apologize or admit wrongdoing, and made a habit of blaming everyone around him if something went wrong. He could not handle criticism or opposition of any kind, and when he received it, retaliated by throwing a temper tantrum and calling people names. He called them "weak and bestial," "stupid and forgetful," "lazy and cowardly."⁵ If he was playing a game and losing, he would quit. When he failed to gain entrance to the Viennese Academy of Art, it was because of the "old-fashioned, fossilized bureaucracy" that had no appreciation for true artistry. He could not grasp how the "racially defiled" Americans beat the Germans in the

---

3. Peter Ross Range, "The Theory of Political Leadership That Donald Trump Shares with Adolf Hitler," *Washington Post*, July 25, 2016, para. 5, https://www.washingtonpost.com/posteverything/wp/2016/07/25/the-theory-of-political-leadership-that-donald-trump-shares-with-adolf-hitler/.

4. Robert G. L. Waite, *The Psychopathic God: Adolf Hitler* (New York: Basic, 1977), 49, as appearing in the Office of Strategic Services (OSS) documents. The OSS documents total 1.2 million pages and shed important historical light on the Holocaust. They are kept in the National Archives.

5. Waite, *Psychopathic God*, 75.

Olympics of 1936, and when he was shown pictures of the Golden Gate Bridge, he responded by demanding that Germany build a bigger one in Hamburg.[6] Every military failure was blamed on one of his generals, but a military success was his alone, and he insisted on being referred to as "The Greatest Commander of All Time."[7]

Arrogance, immaturity, and name-calling are arguably Trump's most notable qualities. He is known for his combative moods and for having to have his own way. When his temper flares, he throws or kicks things. He kicked a chair across a conference room when a project was delayed. He shouted abuse at his construction supervisor, Barbara Res, after he decided he didn't like the cut-rate green marble from China he himself had picked out. He was livid, screaming, "Fucking Ivana! . . . You're making me look bad with all this cheap shit! Who told you to buy this?' He became so enraged, he pulled the door off of an armoire. There was so much anger and rage on his face, Barbara believed he would hit her."[8] His personal mantra, which he has repeated many times, is "When a person screws you, screw them back fifteen times harder."[9] From Camp David, he tweeted out some doozies so utterly ridiculous Steve and I thought for sure they were from a parody account. It was always disturbing to find out they were real. The one that lives on in infamy, as it inspired the Stable Genius Act and the name of a *New York Times* bestseller written by two Pulitzer Prize winners,[10] read:

> I went from VERY successful businessman to top T.V. Star to the President of the United States (on my first try). I think that would qualify as not smart, but genius . . . and a very stable genius at that![11]

A tweet that could have had dire consequences boasted:

> North Korean Leader Kim Jong Un just stated that the "Nuclear Button is on his desk at all times." Will someone from his depleted

---

6. Waite, *Psychopathic God*, 44.

7. Waite, *Psychopathic God*, 17.

8. Barbara A. Res, *Tower of Lies: What My Eighteen Years of Working with Donald Trump Reveals about Him* (Los Angeles: Graymalkin Media, 2020), 229.

9. Kranish and Fisher, *Trump Revealed*, 260.

10. Philip Rucker and Carol Leonnig, *A Very Stable Genius: Donald J. Trump's Testing of America* (New York: Penguin, 2020).

11. Donald J. Trump (@realDonaldTrump), ". . . to President of the United States," Twitter, January 6, 2018, 4:30 a.m., https://twitter.com/realDonaldTrump/status/949619270631256064.

and food starved regime please inform him that I too have a Nuclear Button, but it is a much bigger & more powerful one than his, and my Button works![12]

And in an effort to defend his limited vocabulary,

I'm very highly educated. I know words, I know the best words. But there's no better word than stupid.[13]

In other immature silliness, he made sure the American public knew "there is no problem" with the size of his manhood, during a live presidential debate on national TV.[14]

Charisma

Every sociopathic leader has a certain charisma that draws people in. It has nothing to do with physical attractiveness and everything to do with confidence, passion, and rhetorical power. The clever use of a "larger-than-life" personality was critical to Hitler's success, and it is the element that made his followers fanatically loyal. German citizens listening to Hitler's speeches became mesmerized by his presence. It wasn't that he said anything all that smart or great—it was just that he said what they wanted to hear, and he said it with great confidence and passion as a man who could make it happen. He campaigned on grandiose promises meant to assuage their fears regarding employment stability and a strong economy. Otto Strasser, a German politician and member of the Nazi party, wrote of Hitler's rallies: "His words go like an arrow to their target, he touches each private wound on the raw, liberating the mass unconscious, expressing its innermost aspirations, telling it what it most wants to hear."[15] Hitler's supporters loved him so much, they considered him to be sent by God, as a "savior" who had come to rescue them.

12. Donald J. Trump (@realDonaldTrump), "North Korean Leader Kim Jong Un," Twitter, January 3, 2018, 4:49 p.m., https://twitter.com/realDonaldTrump/status/948355557022420992.

13. "Trump: 'I Have the Best Words,'" *Washington Post*, April 5, 2017, para. 1, https://www.washingtonpost.com/video/national/trump-i-have-the-best-words/2017/04/05/53a9ae4a-19fd-11e7-8598-9a99da559f9e_video.html.

14. "Trump Defends His Manhood after Rubio's 'Small Hands' Comment," *Guardian*, March 3, 2016, https://www.theguardian.com/us-news/video/2016/mar/04/trump-defends-his-manhood-after-rubios-small-hands-comment-video.

15. Waite, *Psychopathic God*, 209.

Donald Trump has a similar magnetism and a way with words that goes straight to the heart of his base. "I am your voice," he says at his rallies. "Believe me. Believe me." Trump's powers of persuasion convinced conservative Christian voters that he would deliver what many of them considered to be a virtual heaven on earth: no more abortions, no gay marriage, strong borders with limited numbers of refugees and immigrants, and overall considerable political influence. He knows how to manipulate people with words.

> The final key to the way I promote is bravado. I play to people's fantasies. People may not always think big themselves, but they can still get very excited by those who do. That's why a little hyperbole never hurts. People want to believe that something is the biggest and greatest and the most spectacular.[16]

One of the most disturbing and insightful boasts he ever made shows that Trump is well aware of his charisma and rhetorical power:

> I have the most loyal voters. I could stand in the middle of Fifth Avenue and shoot somebody [makes shooting gesture toward the camera], and not lose voters.[17]

He often speaks in coded language that appeals to a specific crowd, and his more fanatic followers pick up the "Bat-Signal" and run with it. There can be no doubt that he himself fueled the violence his campaign rallies became known for, since he told his supporters to "knock the crap out of them."[18] There can also be no doubt that his refusal to immediately denounce the KKK and Nazis as the groups solely responsible for the hateful display at Charlottesville was intended to appease them. In fact, the KKK thanked Trump repeatedly for his support.[19] And it was Donald Trump who inspired the insurrectionist mob who stormed the Capitol on January

---

16. Donald J. Trump with Tony Schwartz, *The Art of the Deal* (New York: Random House, 1987), 58.

17. CNN, "Trump Video: I Could Shoot Somebody and Not Lose Voters," YouTube, 00:48, www.youtube.com/watch?v=iTACH1eVIaA.

18. Fabiola Cineas, "Donald Trump Is the Accelerant: A Comprehensive Timeline of Trump Encouraging Hate Groups and Political Violence," *Vox*, January 9, 2021, https://www.vox.com/21506029/trump-violence-tweets-racist-hate-speech.

19. Maria Perez, "KKK Leader David Duke Tweets 'Thank God for Trump! That's Why We Love Him!'," *Newsweek*, November 29, 2017, https://www.newsweek.com/kkk-leader-david-duke-tweets-thank-god-trump-thats-why-we-love-him-726023.

6, 2021. His words to them, fueled by lies about a "stolen election," resulted in millions of dollars worth of damage and the loss of five lives.

> We will never give up. We will never concede, it doesn't happen. You don't concede when there's theft involved. Our country has had enough. We will not take it anymore and that's what this is all about.... We will stop the steal.... The weak Republicans, they're pathetic Republicans and that's what happens.... After this, we're going to walk down and I'll be there with you.... You'll never take back our country with weakness. You have to show strength, and you have to be strong. But we're going to try and give our Republicans, the weak ones, because the strong ones don't need any of our help, we're going to try and give them the kind of pride and boldness that they need to take back our country.[20]

Interestingly enough, for all of his oratorical skill, Hitler did not go unchallenged in his rise to power. In fact, a political crisis developed for him when an anonymous pamphlet circulated *by his own political party* listed many reasons to oppose him. Chiefly among the concerns were his "lust for personal power," his questionable personal finances, expensive tastes, cruel treatment of colleagues, and twisting of facts to suit his own purposes. He was deemed opportunistic and manipulative. The pamphlet appealed to all decent members of the party to refuse to be misled and deceived by what they termed a "megalomaniac and demagogue." It urged a swift removal from office, which we know, unfortunately, went unheeded.[21]

Cruelty and Violence

Donald Trump has an unusual cruel streak, which has been documented from an early age. A Trump neighbor from Queens recalls the time she set her baby in his backyard playpen, went inside for a few moments, and came back out to find that five- or six-year-old Donald was throwing rocks at him. Early classmates and teachers remember Donald as aggressive, surly, mischievous, and a pain. His second grade teacher, whom Donald admits he punched and gave a black eye to, says Donald was "a little shit." One neighbor from Jamaican Estates has never forgotten the "unusual" and

---

20. "Trump's Speech That 'Incited' Capitol Violence: Full Transcript," *Aljazeera*, January 11, 2021, para. 6, https://www.aljazeera.com/news/2021/1/11/full-transcript-donald-trump-january-6-incendiary-speech.

21. Waite, *Psychopathic God*, 209.

"terrifying" act of violence he witnessed when Donald suddenly jumped off his bike and started pummeling another boy. Friends who played baseball with middle-school age Donald concur that he was atypically violent. "He always wanted to hit the ball *through* people. He wanted to overpower them." He absolutely would do anything to win, hated to fail, and one time when he made an out, smashed a borrowed bat on the cement and cracked it. He stomped off in a fury without apologizing to the owner. In high school, classmates at the military academy Trump attended remember him as aggressive, authoritarian, and as someone who would "break" anyone who did not bend to his will. He ordered a cadet to be struck on the back with a broomstick for breaking formation. When his roommate refused to make his bed, Donald grabbed him and tried to push him out of a second-story window, forcing two cadets to intervene to keep him from falling.[22] During his campaign and throughout his presidency, Trump mouthed, "I am going to hurt you," to a protestor and made several other threats from the podium, tweeted out manipulated images of himself pummeling the news media, and regularly shamed and screamed obscenities at his staff.[23]

In regards to his outbursts of anger, Trump has admitted, "I'm a screamer." But Donald Trump's cruel streak extends far beyond physical and vocal aggression. It seems there is no end to the lengths he will go to cause someone pain. According to a classmate at the New York Military Academy, Donald had a thing about rating girls by appearance even back then, and called his date a "dog." In order to hurt Ivana even more during their divorce, he leaked stories to the press, under a false moniker, about how Marla Maples was better in bed. Also in extremely poor taste, he attacked the wife of Ted Cruz during the primaries, tweeting out an unflattering shot of Heidi Cruz next to a picture-perfect Melania with the caption "A picture is worth a thousand words."[24] On stage in front of hundreds of people, Trump humiliated Alicia Machado, and then Chris Christie, for their weight. He physically mocked a handicapped person and a disabled veteran. An entire chapter of this book could be written on Trump's senseless cruelty, but surely the withdrawal of medical insurance coverage for a sick infant tops the list. After Trump's older brother Freddy died of

22. Kranish and Fisher, *Trump Revealed*, 41–42.

23. Dan Merica and Kevin Liptak, "He Cut Your Heart Out: Trump's Anger Proves Memorable," CNN, September 16, 2017, https://www.cnn.com/2017/09/16/politics/trump-anger/index.html.

24. Donald Trump (@realDonaldTrump), "@Don_Vito_08," Twitter, March 23, 2016, 8:55 p.m., https://twitter.com/realDonaldTrump/status/712850174838771712.

alcoholism, Donald promised to help with the medical bills for his brother's new grandson. The baby had a seizure and developed cerebral palsy shortly after birth. But in a shocking display of vindictiveness, Trump withdrew the benefits, which were critical to the infant's care, when his brother's family contested Fred Trump Sr.'s will. Trump admitted that he withdrew the baby's medical insurance for no other reason than he was angry.[25]

It is written that the love of money is the root of all evil, and it is worth noting here that Adolf Hitler also put money before the welfare of his own family. Like Trump, he preferred to paint a picture of himself as a "self-made man," but the truth is that he inherited money from his father's estate at the age of seventeen when his mother died and he became an orphan. From seventeen to twenty-two, he lied about being a student at the Academy of Fine Arts (he actually failed the entrance exam twice) so that he could receive an orphan's pension. This deception deprived his younger sister Paula, only eleven years old, of receiving the full funds that should rightfully have come to her. By court order, he was eventually forced to give up the pension. At this point, he persuaded his crippled aunt to "lend" him large sums of money—which she never got back.[26]

Duplicity

Most sociopaths have a "Jekyll and Hyde" personality. You may be surprised to learn that Hitler's secretaries said he could be quite charming. He brought them chocolates. He went to the opera. He took care of his dying mother. He exchanged pleasantries with people at the bakery he frequented. He was kind to children, taking their hands and praying with them.[27] One moment he would be calm and reasonable, but, as is common in people with personality disorders, if something set him off he would explode into a rage and turn into an uncompromising, ruthless tyrant. From a very young age he used an alter ego called "Wolf." He made his date call him that on an occasion when he felt insecure, but wanted to appear strong, right after he had brutally whipped his dog in front of her.[28] He named several of his military

---

25. Conor Friedersdorf, "Donald Trump's Cruel Streak," *Atlantic*, September 26, 2016, https://www.theatlantic.com/politics/archive/2016/09/donald-trumps-cruel-streak/501554/.

26. Waite, *Psychopathic God*, 196.

27. Waite, *Psychopathic God*, 40.

28. Waite, *Psychopathic God*, 224.

compounds using the moniker—including Wolf's Lair—and also made his younger sister take the name; Paula Hitler became Paula Wolf.

Trump exhibits a similar duplicitousness. With a teleprompter and the right script, Donald Trump earned commendations for acting "presidential." He allowed pastors to pray over him. He visited the Western Wall in Jerusalem. He served food to the victims of Hurricane Harvey. It's the other Trump you have to be careful of. The one with the outrageous temper. The one that flies off the handle when you least expect it. The one who kicks a chair across the conference room. The one who goes off script. The one who promotes violence. The one who speaks in a dizzying display of half-truths, insensible rhetoric, and frequently with his own self-promotion in mind.

For over a decade, Trump called newsrooms pretending to be his own publicist. "John Barron" would give the reporters the latest scoop on The Donald—his sex life, his millions, his businesses, which supermodels wanted to sleep with him, etc. . . . and would also ask them to rate Donald's latest sexual conquest on a scale of one to ten. Someone finally caught on that John Barron and Donald Trump had the same voice, but Trump denied it vehemently. Eventually, a reporter got "John Barron" on tape, and Donald was forced to admit, in court, that it was really him.[29]

Father

Hitler's father was an abusive authoritarian who whistled for his son like a dog and demanded complete obedience. Adolf had to ask permission to speak in his presence. Alois Hitler questioned his son relentlessly on schoolwork and his plans for a career in civil service.[30] He had an explosive temper, whipping Adolf and beating his wife often.[31]

Fred Trump drilled into his son that winning was everything. He told Donald that he needed to become a "killer" in anything he did, and warned him against being "a nothing." (Donald's older brother Freddy was told by his father that his profession as an airline pilot was "nothing," and that he might as well have been a bus driver. Mary Trump attributes Fred's bullying as a main reason her dad died of alcoholism at the age of forty-three.)[32] It

---

29. Michael D'Antonio, "Donald Trump's Long, Strange History of Using Fake Names," *Fortune*, May 18, 2016, http://fortune.com/2016/05/18/donald-trump-fake-names/.

30. Waite, *Psychopathic God*, 173.

31. Waite, *Psychopathic God*, 134.

32. Mary L. Trump, *Too Much and Never Enough: How My Family Created the World's*

is possible that Donald endured some humiliating beatings as well. In the eighth grade, after his father found a hidden cache of knives in Donald's bedroom, he was sent to a strict military school known for breaking its cadets. Physical brutality and verbal abuse were encouraged, and Trump says he had to learn to survive. He recalls being especially roughed up by one of the instructors, who, in Trump's words, was "a fucking prick" who came after him "like you wouldn't believe."[33]

Fearmongering

Hitler was a master at stoking fear. He understood the power of appealing to emotions rather than facts, because he wanted not just supporters but "fanatics." He terrorized them with violent propaganda that played on their every fear and anxiety, especially as it pertained to economic stability. Germany was terrified of communism, so he campaigned largely on fanning the flames of those fears and then convincing German citizens that he was the only one who could put them out.[34]

During his first campaign, Donald Trump painted an ominous picture of a weak, hopeless America in deep distress. Its citizens were unsafe, targeted by swarms of rapists and "barbaric" terrorists, overrun with immigrants trying to take all our money and murder us. In his speeches, America was a disrespected, mismanaged, loser nation led by elitist officials who wanted to pilfer our nation's money away in bad deals to foreign governments. His second campaign, filled with conspiracy theories and threats of socialism and communism, was even worse. Of course, in Trump's dark portrayal of America there was only one source of hope that could put our nation at ease and back on top: him. Some Evangelicals clung to Trump's illusions, helped along by certain cable news networks,[35] while ignoring the words of Jesus: "Watch out for the doomsday deceivers. Many leaders are going to show up with forged identities claiming, 'I'm the One,' or, 'The end is near.' Don't fall for any of that."[36]

Most Dangerous Man (New York: Simon & Schuster, 2020), 65.

33. Kranish and Fisher, *Trump Revealed*, 39.
34. Waite, *Psychopathic God*, 87–88.
35. Amy Sullivan, "America's New Religion: Fox Evangelicalism," *New York Times*, December 15, 2017, https://www.nytimes.com/2017/12/15/opinion/sunday/war-christmas-evangelicals.html.
36. Luke 21:8–9a.

Friendships

Hitler's charisma gained him millions of followers, but he had no personal friends or capacity for true friendship.[37] The people in his life were pawns to be used for gain, and when they ceased to be useful to him, he discarded them.[38] Likewise, Trump has admitted he has no real friends, only business acquaintances, and trusts only his family. Over the course of his presidency he discarded several friendships when they either refused loyalty or ceased to be useful to him, most notably with Rex Tillerson, James Mattis, Dan Coats, and finally, at the bitter end, Michael Cohen, Mick Mulvaney, Bill Barr, and Mike Pence.

Hyperbolic Speech

Hitler's words could not be taken seriously, because he spoke in half-truths, exaggerations, and belligerence. No one was ever sure if he really meant what he said, because so much of what he said was preposterous and irrational.[39] He had a limited vocabulary, repeating favorite words and phrases frequently, and his letters contained grammar and spelling errors that would make a fourth grade teacher cringe. Hitler blamed a childhood teacher, who had given him a bad grade in German and was an "idiot" and "repellent creature."[40]

Besides the other obvious similarities, Trump's spokespeople have indicated that his speech doesn't matter, and that his words should not be taken literally.[41]

Lies

Hitler was a master of deception who prided himself on being, as he called it, "the best actor in Europe." He hid behind many masks. He also lied continually, even about things that could easily be disproved, like where his family

---

37. Waite, *Psychopathic God*, 41.
38. Waite, *Psychopathic God*, 105.
39. Waite, *Psychopathic God*, 83.
40. Waite, *Psychopathic God*, 70.
41. Dalia Lithwick and Robert L. Tsai, "Actually, Paul Ryan, the President's Words Do Matter," *Slate*, December 5, 2016, https://slate.com/news-and-politics/2016/12/paul-ryan-says-it-doesnt-matter-when-trump-lies-on-twitter-thats-garbage.html.

came from. Truth for him was fluid, as he would state facts differently from one moment to the next, depending on how he felt that day.[42]

Trump is a consummate liar, changing his story from one moment to the next. In his first book, *The Art of the Deal*, Trump told his biographer that Ivana was a top model and an alternate on the Czech Olympic ski team,[43] both lies that were easily disproved later. For three days, his campaign denied plagiarizing Michelle Obama's speech, finally issuing a confession only when the media firestorm would not let up.[44] As of this writing, *The Washington Post* has a running list of over thirty thousand false or misleading claims by Donald Trump.[45] Trump himself has admitted that lying is second nature to him. "I play to people's fantasies. . . . It's an innocent form of exaggeration—and a very effective form of promotion."[46]

Literature

Hitler had a massive library of books given to him, but it was for show. He didn't read or attempt to educate himself to gain further knowledge on any topic. When asked, he couldn't name the title of a single book dealing with the social problems he professed to solve in Germany. He said, "My will power is greater than knowledge." On topics he knew nothing about, he spoke in convoluted, and often contradictory, language.[47]

Donald Trump often speaks in "fuzzy" terms about topics he knows nothing about. He has also admitted that he does not read, instead preferring

---

42. Waite, *Psychopathic God*, 35.

43. Jane Mayer, "Donald Trump's Ghostwriter Tells All," *New Yorker*, July 18, 2016, https://www.newyorker.com/magazine/2016/07/25/donald-trumps-ghostwriter-tells-all.

44. Jason Horowitz, "Behind Melania Trump's Cribbed Lines, an Ex-Ballerina Who Loved Writing," *New York Times*, July 20, 2016, https://www.nytimes.com/2016/07/21/us/politics/melania-trump-speech-meredith-mciver.html.

45. Meg Kelly, "Trump's False or Misleading Claims Total 30,573," *Washington Post*, January 24, 2021, https://www.washingtonpost.com/politics/2021/01/24/trumps-false-or-misleading-claims-total-30573-over-four-years/.

46. Trump with Schwartz, *Art of the Deal*, 58.

47. Waite, *Psychopathic God*, 35.

to educate himself by watching "the shows,"[48] or talking to himself.[49] He told a reporter that he had no time to read the biography of any past presidents because he is too busy. He said he doesn't like extensive reports or briefings, either. He would rather have the issues read to him.[50] Only one book has been confirmed—both by Trump and by his ex-wife Ivana—to have rested on his night stand: *Mein Kampf* by Adolf Hitler.[51]

Loyalty

Hitler had an insatiable need for total approval and was driven by a lust for personal power.[52] He demanded complete and total loyalty from his personnel. Either they followed him blindly, or they were traitors.[53] He competed with subordinates and could not tolerate the idea of someone being superior to him or getting in his way. Under Hitler's regime, the armed forces were taught to take an oath not to their country, but to one man:

> I swear by God this sacred oath, that I will render unconditional obedience to Adolf Hitler, The Führer of the German Reich and people, Supreme Commander of the Armed Forces, and will be ready as a brave soldier to risk my life at any time for this oath.[54]

Donald Trump has a long history of demanding loyalty and also of threatening people who stand in his way or speak ill of him. A sternly

---

48. Chuck Todd, "Meet the Press Transcript—August 16, 2015," NBC, August 16, 2015, https://www.nbcnews.com/meet-the-press/meet-press-transcript-august-16-2015-n412636.

49. Joe Scarborough and Mika Brzezinski, "Morning Joe," MSNBC, March 16, 2016, https://factba.se/transcript/donald-trump-interview-msnbc-morning-joe-march-16-2016. When asked with whom he consults about foreign policy issues, Trump said, "I'm speaking with myself, number one, because I have a very good brain and I've said a lot of things."

50. David A Graham, "The President Who Doesn't Read," *Atlantic*, January 5, 2018, https://www.theatlantic.com/politics/archive/2018/01/americas-first-post-text-president/549794/.

51. "Donald Trump's Ex-Wife Once Said Trump Kept a Book of Hitler's Speeches by His Bed," *Business Insider*, September 1, 2015, https://www.businessinsider.com/donald-trumps-ex-wife-once-said-he-kept-a-book-of-hitlers-speeches-by-his-bed-2015-8.

52. Waite, *Psychopathic God*, 53.

53. Waite, *Psychopathic God*, 33.

54. Waite, *Psychopathic God*, 81, as appearing in the OSS documents.

worded letter from John Bassett, the owner of the Tampa Bay Bandits, with whom Trump had a disagreement in 1984, reads:

> Dear Donald, I have listened with astonishment at your personal abuse of the commissioner and various of your partners if they did not happen to espouse one of your causes or agree with one of your arguments. . . . You are bigger, younger, and stronger than I, which means I'll have no regrets whatsoever punching you right in the mouth the next time an instance occurs where you personally scorn me, or anyone else, who does not happen to salute and dance to your tune.[55]

Richard Ravitch, who was the chairman for the Urban Development Corporation when Trump was trying to build a Hyatt in New York, was also astonished at the young developer's threats and brashness. When Ravitch refused to give Trump a tax break for which he did not qualify, Trump vowed to have him fired. (When asked about it later, Trump denied the account and called Ravitch an "overrated person.")[56]

Trump also employs a public relations strategy that is well known among the news media. First he bribes the reporter, and then he demands favorable stories. This practice dates way back. In the late seventies, when he was first starting out, Donald Trump worked the press to build a name for himself as a self-made visionary. But an investigative journalist named Wayne Barrett was hired by the *Village Voice* to do a different story—the story of a privileged son using his father's political connections to get the inside track on real estate deals in a corrupt New York. When Barrett started digging into the records related to Trump dealings, he was astonished to receive a personal phone call from Trump himself. Trump said he wanted to be friends. Then he offered Barrett an apartment. When it was refused, Trump threatened him by saying, "I've broken one writer. I really value my reputation and I don't hesitate to sue." Barrett wasn't swayed. He was the first among many to publish an account of the influence Fred Trump's political connections had on Donald Trump's business

---

55. Matt Bonesteel, "Donald Trump Was Such a USFL Bully that a Fellow Owner Threatened to Punch Him," *Washington Post*, March 3, 2016, para. 4, https://www.washingtonpost.com/news/early-lead/wp/2016/03/03/donald-trump-was-such-a-usfl-bully-that-a-fellow-owner-threatened-to-punch-him/.

56. Kranish and Fisher, *Trump Revealed*, 76.

endeavors, as well as the suspicious favors granted him by government and bankruptcy court officials.[57]

Messiah Complex

Psychopathic leaders very often believe themselves to be chosen by a Higher Power. Hitler truly believed, and convinced his followers, that he was chosen by God as a savior for Germany.[58] He wanted to be remembered as "The Greatest Man in History" and used that expression when speaking of himself. He liked to mention that he came to power at age thirty, the same age another Messiah started his ministry.[59]

Trump uses similar verbiage and has made repeated claims that he is the one and only person who can save our nation. "I alone can fix it,"[60] he has said. "I will give you everything. I will give you what you've been looking for for 50 years. I'm the only one."[61] Trump biographer Michael D'Antonio concurs, Donald Trump believes that he is "genetically gifted" for the presidency.[62] Eerily, shortly after Trump was elected, the Republican National Committee sent out a Christmas card referencing our Savior's birth with a thinly veiled celebration in honor of "a new King."[63] They walked it back the next day, after online outrage.

Racism

Hitler was an Aryan who believed that white people were God's pure, chosen race and that non-Aryans were contaminated by polluted blood. He attended the Roman Catholic Church, recited Scripture, prayed with

---

57. Kranish and Fisher, *Trump Revealed*, 102–5.
58. Waite, *Psychopathic God*, 16.
59. Waite, *Psychopathic God*, 205.
60. Range, "Theory of Political Leadership."
61. Steve Benen, "Trump Says He's 'the Only One' Who Can Protect the US," MSNBC, October 12, 2016, para. 2, https://www.msnbc.com/rachel-maddow-show/trump-says-hes-the-only-one-who-can-protect-the-us-msna912406.
62. Michael D'Antonio, "Who Is Donald Trump?," CNN, July 10, 2016, para. 47, http://www.cnn.com/2016/07/10/opinions/donald-trump-biography-michael-dantonio/.
63. Mahita Gajanan, "The RNC Says Its Christmas Message about a 'New King' Referred to Jesus, Not Donald Trump," *Time*, December 25, 2016, https://time.com/4617878/rnc-donald-trump-christmas-new-king/.

people, and all the while insisted that "the Jew is the personification of the Devil and of all evil." Thus he felt justified that he was doing the will of God.[64] It was rumored that Hitler's paternal grandmother conceived Hitler's father after having been raped by a Jewish man. This allegation worried Hitler to such a degree that he used leeches periodically to suck out his blood.[65] He was terrified of infectious diseases, and many of his speeches were riddled with terms about disease, infections, and blood poisoning, and—his most feared disease of all—syphilis, which was something he believed was contracted from "Jews and Negroes."[66]

According to his official biographer, Michael D'Antonio, Donald Trump also has an irrational fear and loathing of people who do not look like him. Trump has warned that what Hispanics bring to America is "like vomit," and he is under the impression that they bring "tremendous infectious diseases . . . across the border."[67] He called Haitians and African nations "shithole countries,"[68] and the mostly Black Baltimore "disgusting, rat and rodent infested," a "dangerous place," where "no human being would want to live."[69] Born and raised in Baltimore, journalist Victor Blackwell observed, "Donald Trump has tweeted more than 43,000 times, he's insulted thousands of people, many different types of people, but when he tweets about infestation, it's about black and brown people."[70]

Fred Trump, Donald Trump, and Trump Management, Inc. were sued by the federal government in 1973 for "refusing to rent and negotiate rentals with Blacks, requiring different rental terms and conditions because of race, and misrepresenting that apartments were not available."

64. Waite, *Psychopathic God*, 29.
65. Waite, *Psychopathic God*, 128.
66. Waite, *Psychopathic God*, 24.
67. Rupert Neate and Jo Tuckman, "Donald Trump: Mexican Migrants Bring 'Tremendous Infectious Disease' to US," *Guardian*, July 6, 2015, para. 1, https://www.theguardian.com/us-news/2015/jul/06/donald-trump-mexican-immigrants-tremendous-infectious-disease.
68. Ali Vitali et al., "Trump Referred to Haiti and African Nations as 'Shithole' Countries," NBC, January 10, 2018, https://www.nbcnews.com/politics/white-house/trump-referred-haiti-african-countries-shithole-nations-n836946.
69. Donald J. Trump (@realDonaldTrump), ". . . As proven last week," Twitter, July 27, 2019, 4:14 a.m., https://twitter.com/realDonaldTrump/status/1155073965880172544.
70. Wilborn P. Nobles III, "Trump Calls Baltimore 'Disgusting . . . Rodent Infested Mess,' Rips Rep. Elijah Cummings Over Border Criticism," *Baltimore Sun*, July 27, 2019, para. 21, www.baltimoresun.com/politics/bs-md-pol-cummings-trump-20190727-chty2yovtvfzfcjkeaui7wm5zi-story.html.

The government offered evidence that Trump employees were instructed to mark a *c* for "colored" on top of the application every time a Black person applied. The Trump employee who came forward about the racist practices feared for his life—he said if the Trumps found out who it was, they "would have him knocked off." The lawsuit was eventually settled, and Fred and Donald Trump were forced to sign a consent order, but three years later the Justice Department accused them of failure to comply and of continuing to make their apartments unavailable to Black persons.[71]

Trump seems to have a special knack for inflaming racial tension and tapping into white supremacist bigotry. In 1989, he took out a full-page ad in the *New York Times* calling for the death penalty for five teenagers, four Black and one Hispanic, for the rape and beating of a woman in Central Park. Donald wrote:

> Mayor Koch has stated that hate and rancor should be removed from our hearts. I do not think so. I want to hate these muggers and murderers. They should be forced to suffer and, when they kill, they should be executed for their crimes. . . . Yes, Mayor Koch, I want to hate these murderers and I always will. I am not looking to psychoanalyze them or understand them, I am looking to punish them. . . . I no longer want to understand their anger. I want them to understand our anger. I want them to be afraid.[72]

According to his niece Mary, Trump's denouncement was "unvarnished racism meant to stir up racial animosity in a city already seething with it. All five boys, Kevin Richardson, Antron McCray, Raymond Santana, Korey Wise, and Yusef Salaam, were subsequently cleared, proven innocent via incontrovertible DNA evidence. To this day, however, Donald insists that they were guilty—yet another example of his inability to drop a preferred narrative even when it's contradicted by established fact."[73]

Trump also stirred up controversy on Capitol Hill, when he questioned whether his casino-owning competitors in Atlantic City were really Native Americans, because "they don't look like Indians to me."[74]

71. Kranish and Fisher, *Trump Revealed*, 66.

72. "Bring Back the Death Penalty," *New York Times*, May 1, 1989, para. 3, http://apps.frontline.org/clinton-trump-keys-to-their-characters/pdf/trump-newspaper.pdf.

73. Mary Trump, *Too Much*, 204.

74. "'They Don't Look Like Indians to Me': Donald Trump on Native American Casinos in 1993," *Washington Post*, July 1, 2016, 3:58, https://www.washingtonpost.com/video/politics/they-dont-look-like-indians-to-me-donald-trump-on-native-american-casinos-in-1993/2016/07/01/20736038-3fd4-11e6-9e16-4cf01a41decb_video.html.

NBC kicked him off *The Apprentice* because of his derogatory statements toward immigrants. Besides calling people from Mexico "rapists," he accused Judge Curiel, who was presiding over the Trump University lawsuit, of being an "unfair Mexican." Trump also equated Nazis and KKK members with protestors during the Charlottesville rally. During his campaign, he did not immediately denounce the backing of the KKK, and claimed at first that he didn't know who David Duke was.[75]

This being the case, white supremacists with "KKK FOR TRUMP" signs stood loud and proud at his rallies. Trump supporters were overheard telling Black people to "go back to Africa." Two days after a Black protestor was punched in the mouth at one of his rallies, Trump gave his approval, stating such attacks on protesters were "very, very appropriate" and the kind of action "we need a little bit more of."[76] Trump is quoted as saying that "laziness is a trait in blacks," wouldn't allow Black men to count the money at his casinos,[77] complained that Black men and Native Americans have an advantage over white men in our country, and pardoned Sheriff Joe Arpaio, a man convicted of severe crimes against immigrants, who faced jail time for criminal contempt.[78]

Rallies

Hitler loved a good rally. He wanted people to envy his position of power, and he wanted to overtake them with his words and promises. He craved people's attention and adoration of him, and often came off the stage soaked in sweat, physically and emotionally exhausted.[79] It is written by a childhood playmate that he was a compulsive and aggressive talker even in boyhood, that he would control every game, and that he would be friends only

---

75. Camila Domonoske, "Trump Fails to Condemn KKK on Television, Turns to Twitter to Clarify," NPR, February 28, 2016, https://www.npr.org/sections/thetwo-way/2016/02/28/468455028/trump-wont-condemn-kkk-says-he-knows-nothing-about-white-supremacists.

76. Cineas, "Donald Trump Is the Accelerant."

77. Ben Mathis-Lilley, "'Laziness Is a Trait in Blacks,' 1991 Book Quotes Trump as Saying," *Slate*, July 20, 2016, https://slate.com/news-and-politics/2016/07/trump-complained-about-blacks-inherent-laziness-1991-book-says.html.

78. Colin Dwyer, "Ex-Sheriff Joe Arpaio Convicted of Criminal Contempt," NPR, July 31, 2017, https://www.npr.org/sections/thetwo-way/2017/07/31/540629884/ex-sheriff-joe-arpaio-convicted-of-criminal-contempt.

79. Waite, *Psychopathic God*, 53.

with people he could dominate.[80] His favorite thing was to watch people fall under his power and chant his name. Robert Waite writes that as Hitler led them, the crowds became mesmerized:

> The massed ranks of the faithful, eyes aflame with passion, roared back the mindless chant: Sieg Heil! Ein Volk! Ein Reich! Ein Führer![81]

Needless to say, Trump has a similar affinity for rallies, and to hear his name chanted back to him: "Trump! Trump! Trump!" He held an unprecedented number of rallies while in office—many for no apparent reason. It has been reported that he "gets very excited" as he "feeds off the energy of the crowd," and loves to talk so much that he has a hard time sticking with the script. Against the advice of his staff and the mayor of Phoenix, Trump held a Make America Great Again rally right after the horrible events of Charlottesville, when the country was still in shock. He fired the event coordinator the next day because he was unhappy with the crowd size.[82]

He has an obvious knack for self-promotion, and it has been surmised that having a workaholic father and a sickly mother contributed to Donald's insatiable need for attention. While they were still married, Ivana was asked to sum up the Donald she knew. After a brief pause, her assessment was "I think he's a little boy who didn't get enough attention and has been seeking attention ever since."[83] President Trump rudely pushed the prime minister of Montenegro out of the way at NATO headquarters, so that he could be in front for the cameras.[84] "The show is Trump," he said, during his *Playboy* interview, "and it is sold-out performances everywhere."[85]

---

80. Waite, *Psychopathic God*, 147.

81. Waite, *Psychopathic God*, 84, as appearing in the OSS documents.

82. Margaret Hartmann, "Trump Fires Longtime Event Organizer over Sparse Crowd at Phoenix Rally," *New York Intelligencer*, August 29, 2017, https://nymag.com/intelligencer/2017/08/trump-fires-event-organizer-over-crowd-size-at-phoenix-rally.html.

83. D'Antonio, "Who Is Donald Trump?," para. 75.

84. Daniella Diaz, "Watch President Trump Push a Prime Minister Aside," CNN, May 25, 2017, https://www.cnn.com/2017/05/25/politics/trump-pushes-prime-minister-nato-summit/index.html.

85. Glenn Plaskin, "The 1990 *Playboy* Interview with Donald Trump," *Playboy Magazine*, March 1, 1990, https://www.ebroadsheet.com/wp-content/uploads/2017/03/playboy-interview-donald-trump-1990.

Patriotism

Hitler wanted to make his country strong because he saw it as a reflection of himself. If another country rose up against him, he immediately threatened to "smash" them with military action. He considered everything in life as a battle you could either win or lose, and he needed to win. He demanded that his personnel be completely subordinate and that military success be guaranteed. His military failures toward the end of the war were blamed on betrayal of his own army. His main political ideologies were: exaltation of the Führer and the demise of democracy, militarism and war, anti-Semitism and racism, propaganda, and use of terror to force a nation to do the will of one man.[86]

Despite his bone spurs, tax dodging, and attacks on war heroes and veterans, Donald Trump pretends to be the consummate patriot. He once hugged and kissed the American flag at a rally. He is a fan of forced patriotism, as evidenced by calling NFL players who kneeled "sons of bitches" and demanding they stand. He is a fan of Vladimir Putin, whom he refers to as "nice," "smart," and "strong." He seemingly admires Putin's evil, authoritarian regime, and tweeted, "Will he become my new best friend?"[87]

Sense of Humor

Hitler didn't have one, at least not about himself. He had an intense fear of being laughed at.[88] He did, however, like to embarrass and humiliate people as a "joke," including making fun of a one-armed publisher and an assistant press director who was deaf.[89]

Mary Trump tells of a time when her dad, Freddy, who was tired of being bullied by Donald, dumped a bowl of mashed potatoes on his head, and the whole table laughed. Donald was mortified and to this day has not gotten over the shame and embarrassment. When her aunt Maryanne jokingly brought it up at a family dinner in 2017, Trump grimaced, crossed his arms, and refused to acknowledge her.[90]

---

86. Waite, *Psychopathic God*, 89.

87. Donald J. Trump (@realDonaldTrump), "Do you think Putin," Twitter, June 18, 2013, 8:17 p.m., https://twitter.com/realDonaldTrump/status/347191326112112640.

88. Waite, *Psychopathic God*, 13–14.

89. Waite, *Psychopathic God*, 9.

90. Mary Trump, *Too Much*, 7.

Trump was proudly at the helm of the birther movement against President Obama, insisting that he had been born in Kenya, hinting that he had hired private investigators to look into it. He offered $5 million to whomever could provide Obama's college transcripts and passport information. After the birth certificate was brought forth and put on display, Obama tried to make light of the situation and made Trump the butt of some of his jokes at the White House Correspondents' dinner.[91] It's been speculated that Trump has been attempting to destroy Obama's legacy ever since.

Sexual Perversion/Misogyny

Hitler was into pornography, talked about sex constantly, made lewd and degrading comments about women, and had a preference for much younger women. Six of the seven women he was intimate with committed or attempted suicide. One of them was his niece, Geli, who was nineteen years his junior and only seventeen when they began their relationship. She shot and killed herself with the Führer's own pistol when she was twenty-three.[92] Hitler idealized women and at the same time sought to degrade them. To be admired, a woman must stay in the background, be "perfectly formed," and never disagree with him on anything. A woman who challenged him immediately invited his wrath. One of Hitler's secretaries wrote that Adolf Hitler lacked basic humanity. She said, "He was like a shell with no soul."[93]

Donald Trump owned a strip club, appeared in a soft-core porn video, had affairs with porn stars and Playboy Bunnies and has made countless vulgar comments publicly about women and sex. Trump has stated, "No one likes women more than I do." Conversely, his stories led one reporter to conclude of Trump's attitude toward women: "You have to treat them like s---."[94]

---

91. CNN, "Watch Obama Roast Trump," YouTube, April 30, 2011, https://www.youtube.com/watch?v=HHckZCxdRkA.

92. Waite, *Psychopathic God*, 233, 241.

93. Waite, *Psychopathic God*, 49.

94. Julie Baumgold, "Fighting Back: Trump Scrambles Off the Canvas," *New York Magazine*, November 9, 1992, 36–46, esp. 41.

Wealth

Adolf Hitler loved money and was excessively wealthy. However, when he came into power, it was found that he didn't pay his taxes. He also frequently refused to pay people what he owed them.[95]

Donald Trump pledged to disclose his "very big . . . very beautiful" tax returns, but of course did not. He has bragged about not paying taxes and getting away with paying as little as possible, calling it "the American way."[96] A September 2020 report in *The New York Times*, which obtained tax records with the aid of Mary Trump, revealed that he paid only $750 in federal taxes the year he was elected and owes $450 million to creditors.[97] In January of 2023, the Trump Organization was fined $1.6 million following a tax fraud conviction.[98]

He has a long history of scamming people. Besides the Trump University scheme, Trump companies "have been involved in more than 100 tax disputes, and the New York State Department of Finance has obtained liens on Trump properties for unpaid tax bills at least three dozen times."[99] Hundreds of lawsuits have been filed against him by people he employed but then refused to pay—real estate brokers, lawyers, construction crews, lobbying firms, and other vendors. One business owner, Mark Cutler, was overjoyed when his sign company won the contract to make the neon TRUMP TAJ MAHAL sign. But after it was completed, Trump refused to pay, instead offering him one third of what was due. Even after depleting his daughter's college fund, Cutler could not absorb the losses, couldn't pay his employees, and couldn't order promised materials for

---

95. Waite, *Psychopathic God*, 196.

96. Dan Mangan, "Trump Brags about Not Paying Taxes: 'That Makes Me Smart,'" CNBC, September 26, 2016, https://www.cnbc.com/2016/09/26/trump-brags-about-not-paying-taxes-that-makes-me-smart.html.

97. Russ Buettner et al., "The President's Taxes: Long Concealed Records Show Trump's Chronic Losses and Years of Tax Avoidance," *New York Times*, September 27, 2020, https://www.nytimes.com/interactive/2020/09/27/us/donald-trump-taxes.html.

98. Dareh Gregorian and Adam Reiss, "Trump Organization Fined $1.6 Million for Long-Running Tax Fraud Scheme," NBC, January 13, 2023, https://www.nbcnews.com/politics/donald-trump/trump-organization-faces-sentencing-tax-fraud-scheme-rcna65013.

99. Nick Penzenstadler and Susan Page, "Trump's 3,500 Lawsuits Unprecedented for a Presidential Nominee," *USA Today*, June 1, 2016, para. 6, https://www.usatoday.com/story/news/politics/elections/2016/06/01/donald-trump-lawsuits-legal-battles/84995854/.

other customers. His association with Donald Trump turned into financial devastation for Mark, his company, his employees, and his family, and he ended up filing for bankruptcy.[100]

Another high-profile case from the 1980s involved hundreds of undocumented Polish immigrants hired to demolish Bonwit Teller, a Fifth Avenue department store that had to be destroyed to make room for Trump Tower. Using sledgehammers and blowtorches, the "Polish brigade" worked for several months, twelve- to eighteen-hour days, seven days a week, without hard hats. They often slept on the concrete floor. They were paid less than five dollars an hour, sometimes in vodka. Many went unpaid, and if they complained, were threatened with deportation. Three years later, a lawsuit for the back wages Trump owed them was filed. The immigration lawyer who represented the workers said that a representative from Trump's organization—a "Mr. Barron"—had threatened a counter-lawsuit if the workers didn't drop their demand for back payments. The threat didn't work. The judge ruled against Trump, and the case was settled and sealed in 1999.[101] For a man who claims that he "never" settles lawsuits, Trump has settled with plaintiffs—in some cases as high as hundreds of thousands of dollars—in at least one hundred cases.[102] In 2024, Trump was penalized $454 million by the city of New York for fraudulently inflating his net worth in order to dupe lenders. The judge noted that his "complete lack of contrition and remorse borders on pathological."[103]

The False Leader

Some world leaders are positioned by God and are specially graced as influencers of love, mercy, freedom, and justice. They propel society forward with the type of leadership they convey. A person graced by God for this type of leadership has a positive, self-disciplined, contagious, forward-thinking energy about them. Dr. Martin Luther King Jr., Nelson Mandela, Malala Yousafzai, and Ellen Johnson Sirleaf come to mind. Second Timothy 1:7 says a person graced by the Holy Spirit is marked

---

100. Kranish and Fisher, *Trump Revealed*, 202–3.
101. Kranish and Fisher, *Trump Revealed*, 85–87.
102. Penzenstadler and Page, "Trump's 3,500 Lawsuits."
103. Kevin Breuninger, "Trump Ordered to Pay $454 Million in Fines and Interest in NY Business Fraud Case," CNBC, February 16, 2024, https://www.cnbc.com/2024/02/16/trump-fraud-trial-judge-engoron-verdict-ny-ag-business-case.html.

by love, a sound mind, and possession of self-control. A person led by the Holy Spirit brings peace into the room with them, even in stressful situations. A person led by the Holy Spirit has a great capacity for humility and friendship and mutual respect. A person led by the Holy Spirit speaks encouraging words of life. A person led by the Holy Spirit has joy. A person led by the Holy Spirit is gentle and patient and kind. A person led by the Holy Spirit has courage, doesn't need to blame other people, and doesn't need to compete for attention.

A false leader is someone who attains a position of leadership not by God's grace, but by false, dangerous circumstances. They are self-exalting grumblers who follow their own desires while boasting about themselves and flattering others for their own advantage. They divide instead of unite, follow their own base instincts, and are not led by the Holy Spirit.[104] The Bible calls these leaders *false prophets*. "But there were also false prophets among the people, just as there will be false teachers among you.... Many will follow their depraved conduct and will bring the way of truth into disrepute. In their greed these teachers will exploit you with fabricated stories."[105] A false leader gains power by telling you everything you want to hear.

It's important—moreover, it's *biblical*—to never assess a leader (spiritual, political, or otherwise) based solely on the "good things" he is doing or promises to do. Keith Raniere did good things for his community before he was sent to prison for sex-trafficking and racketeering. David Miscavige does good things for society under the umbrella of Scientology. L. Ron Hubbard and Jim Jones did good things too. But all of them are false leaders, and all of them eventually led their communities into chaos, division, and violence.

If you want to know whether a leader is placed by God or not, conduct the test of spirits. Check the spiritual atmosphere around them, as it stands most of the time. How do they generally treat people? The test of spirits is not determined by the promises they make or the prophecies given about them. It isn't whether they are Republican or Democrat, conservative or liberal. The test is not whether the leader makes decisions that the white evangelical church in America agrees with. The test is the overwhelming presence of good spirits—or bad spirits—in their life. We can be sure that a person who is routinely hateful, cruel, destructive, divisive, and violent

---

104. Jude 16–19.
105. 2 Pet 2:1–2.

is not being led by God. A leader who frequently and erratically lashes out with his tongue, lies profusely, and brings chaos and paranoia into the room with him is not led by God. If he craves constant praise and attention and loyalty, he is not led by God. The leader may possess a powerful energy that will at first make his followers feel similarly powerful, but eventually it will unleash lies, disruption, paranoia, and rage onto the people he leads. They will feel angry and fearful much of the time, and possibly even violent. A person led by a false leader may feel it is necessary to bully and radicalize others into their position.

Adolf Hitler was a psychopath who had a demonic, antichrist spirit using him to exterminate Jewish people and others he judged "contaminated" and "inferior." He was also a mentally disturbed and unstable politician whose sociopathic tendencies contributed to his rise in power and ultimately affected his public policy. The thing is, he acted like a lunatic only some of the time. The rest of the time, he seemed normal.

Such is often the case with a false leader.

10

Grabbing Anything

"When you're a star, they let you do it."—Donald Trump[1]

When the *Access Hollywood* tape came out, I was mentoring two young ladies from my home church who were in the midst of drug addiction as a result of childhood sexual abuse. We met together every other week or so to pray, to read Scripture, and to talk about Jesus's great love for them. While we prayed, I held their hands, and I felt the extreme love of Jesus coursing through me. I asked the Holy Spirit to pour that love and acceptance into the deepest part of their hearts. I prayed that Christ's love would overwhelm the residual despair and break the shame that had built up as a result of the abuse. I tried to listen to God so I could speak words of healing that would counter the words and tone of the enemy. Jesus's voice is replete with love and honor, and he speaks in a way that restores dignity to the hearer. His voice is the exact opposite of what the voice of the enemy sounds like.

> I did try and f*** her. She was married. I moved on her like a bitch. But I couldn't get there. And she was married. Then all of a sudden I see her, she's now got the big phony tits and everything. She's totally changed her look. Whoa! Whoa! Yeah, that's her. With the gold. I better use some Tic Tacs just in case I start kissing her. You know, I'm automatically attracted to beautiful—I just start kissing them. It's like a magnet. Just kiss. I don't even wait. And when

1. Makela, "Transcript."

you're a star, they let you do it. You can do anything.... Grab them by the p*ssy. You can do anything ...

It looks good.... Oh nice legs huh. Oof, get out of the way, honey. Oh, that's good legs. Go ahead ... Melania said this was OK.[2]

So when I heard Donald Trump brag about sexually assaulting women, and in such blatant, shocking terms, I didn't just hear Donald. I heard the enemy, who hates women, growling from the deepest pit in hell—and I took it personally. I cried, and then I got very, very angry. I went up to my bedroom, got my Bible, and went face down before the Lord and cast my considerable grievances onto him. I told him exactly what I thought of Trump and his low, misogynistic view of women. I waited to hear what God had to say. For some reason, I felt like reading Jude. Now, I don't spend a lot of time in the book of Jude. It's not a book that comes to mind often or to which I would typically go for comfort. At the time I felt led to read it, I couldn't have even told you what it was about. But I turned to it anyway. I had just gotten a Message version of the Bible, and my jaw about dropped on the floor when I read these words:

> Dear friends, I've dropped everything to write you about this life of salvation that we have in common. I have to write insisting—begging!—that you fight with everything you have in you for this faith entrusted to us as a gift to guard and cherish. What has happened is that some people have infiltrated our ranks (our Scriptures warned us this would happen), who beneath their pious skin are shameless scoundrels. Their design is to replace the sheer grace of our God with sheer license—which means doing away with Jesus Christ, our one and only Master.[3]

> This is exactly the same program of these latest infiltrators: dirty sex, rule and rulers thrown out, glory dragged in the mud.[4]

> These people are warts on your love feasts as you worship and eat together. They're giving you a black eye—carousing shamelessly, *grabbing anything that isn't nailed down.*[5]

Rarely has the word of God spoken to me with so much clarity. The phrasing was too much of a coincidence for me to cast aside. God had

2. Makela, "Transcript."
3. Jude 3–4.
4. Jude 8.
5. Jude 12; emphasis added.

GRABBING ANYTHING

heard my anguish, and he was answering me. I stopped crying and read through the passage again, more carefully. Jude was clearly worked up. He wanted to warn the church about something, and he wasn't pulling any punches. Careless scoundrels had entered the church under false pretenses. They wanted to get a foot in the door with the true followers of Christ, so that they could use them to their own advantage. They had no intention of following the Holy Spirit. They followed their own base instincts and did what they felt like doing. Ultimately, they were rejecting God and his rightful authority, all while pretending to be interested in him. But their behavior—engaging in dirty sex, and carousing and grabbing shamelessly—spoke loud and clear.

Jude's warning to the church was severe. He didn't want the people of God to be charmed by the grandiose promises of a pretender. "These are the complainers, the bellyachers, grabbing for the biggest piece of the pie, talking big, saying anything they think will get them ahead."[6] According to Jude, the church had a responsibility in this. God had given them a solemn duty to guard and to cherish their faith, and with that, their reputation. King Solomon wrote, "A good reputation and respect are worth much more than silver and gold. . . . When you see trouble coming, don't be stupid and walk right into it—be smart and hide."[7]

Jude saw trouble coming. The church's association with these "shameless scoundrels" would tarnish their reputation and undermine their witness to the world. An alliance with this type of person would ultimately lead to their detriment. Jude went on to warn them that the pretenders will be judged by God for every way they have exploited his name, and Christianity, for their own personal gain.

> But remember, dear friends, that the apostles of our Master, Jesus Christ, told us this would happen: "In the last days there will be people who don't take these things seriously anymore. They'll treat them like a joke, and make a religion of their own whims and lusts." These are the ones who split churches, thinking only of themselves. There's nothing to them, no sign of the Spirit![8]

The pretenders that Jude warns of here have no sign of the Holy Spirit, and no actual fear of God. They are just using God's name, and relationships with his people, to make their own name great.

6. Jude 16.
7. Prov 22:1–3 CEV.
8. Jude 17–19.

Every time Donald Trump belittled a woman's appearance, every time he told another bold-faced lie, every time he retweeted a conspiracy theory, every time he failed to stand up for people of color, every time he stirred up racism and division, every time he insulted a national hero, every time he demonized immigrants, every time he tried to undermine the free press, every time he advocated violence on his own behalf—he was mocking God. He was saying, "OK, church, you gonna do anything about it?" And our silent approval said, "No, sir. We would rather have what you can give us." We were acquiescing to the enemy, and we were doing it in God's holy name.

Donald Trump pretended to be a "baby" believer, and then he used his high position, partially attained by that very claim, to abuse and shame and dehumanize people, and to promote violence. God will not be mocked. Let it be known here, today, that God expects people who have claimed repentance and have professed his holy name to have at least a modicum of change in character to show for it. One may not profess Christ at the same time he is calling a woman "bimbo, crazy, low I.Q." via tweet from the Oval Office. A person who pretends he wants to follow God, but actually just wants to hide behind God's name to exalt his own, does nothing but make God angry.

> And that means killing off everything connected with that way of death: sexual promiscuity, impurity, lust, doing whatever you feel like whenever you feel like it, and grabbing whatever attracts your fancy. That's a life shaped by things and feelings instead of by God. It's because of this kind of thing that God is about to explode in anger. It wasn't long ago that you were doing all that stuff and not knowing any better. But you know better now, so make sure it's all gone for good: bad temper, irritability, meanness, profanity, dirty talk.[9]

Trump's rage, malice, profane speech, slander, and calls for violence remained throughout his time in the Oval Office because he never had any intention of actually obeying God. He was only using God's name to do what he does best—grab anything he could get his hands on, including the presidency. The church may have been fooled, but God wasn't.

According to the book of Jude, the people of God will find that, in the end, it is counterproductive to the gospel to align with a pretender who sneers at what he can't understand, claims to be "the best thing that

---

9. Col 3:5–8.

ever happened to Christianity"[10] while continuing to do whatever he feels like doing, grabs for the biggest piece of the pie, and says anything he can think of to get ahead. Moreover, per Jude, the church should have some regard for its own reputation.

May we never again remain silent while a man posing as a "baby Christian" drags God's glory through the mud.[11]

---

10. Alia Shoab, "Donald Trump Told a Christian Network That 'Nobody Had Done More for Christianity or for Religion Itself' Than Him," *Business Insider*, October 3, 2021, https://www.businessinsider.com/donald-trump-said-that-nobody-has-done-more-for-religion-than-him-2021-10.

11. "This is exactly the same program of these latest infiltrators: dirty sex, rule and rulers thrown out, glory dragged in the mud" (Jude 8).

11

The Contaminated Gospel

A good person who gives in to a bad person is like a muddied spring, a polluted well.—Prov 25:26

My culinary skills are not great even when I *am* concentrating on the recipe, but my family teases me that when I'm in the middle of a writing project, it's best if I just stay out of the kitchen altogether. I'm prone to putting something on the stove and then dashing off to jot down some thoughts while it burns or boils over. Many family meals have been scorched by "Mama's book." While writing *Six Years in the Hanoi Hilton*, I was once so distracted making homestyle macaroni and cheese that I confused the measurement for the macaroni with the measurement for the bread crumb topping. I didn't realize it until I went to serve it later, and by then it was too late. I hoped no one would notice. After a few bites of what could only be described as breadcrumbs covered with melted cheese, and a lot of giggles, my kids asked what we were eating. My husband suggested we call it "macaroni surprise," because for every few bites of cheesy crumbs you'd get—*surprise!*—an actual macaroni.

So it wasn't shocking that, while writing this book, I put a homemade pizza in the oven and forgot about it. (And by "homemade," I mean I purchased a frozen pizza and put a handful of spinach and kalamata olives on top.) I smelled it burning and raced downstairs to beat the smoke alarm, but I was too late. Some of my toppings had fallen off and burned to a crisp on the floor of the oven, and when I opened the oven door, I was accosted by a thick layer of smoke and black particles of burned veggies, bursting to make their escape. I coughed and then I stood up, and in the sunlight coming in from the kitchen window I could barely make out the charred debris dancing in the sunlight, floating gracefully into my hair, on my shirt, and onto my counters. When I tried to wipe up the tiny specks, they spread around and left long gray smudge lines all over my shiny white countertops. "What a perfect illustration," I thought, "for what I was just writing about. Contamination in the air that is hard to see until the light shines in."

The Contaminating Yeast

The gospel of Jesus is pure and holy and lovely and eternal. It is the good news of God's kingdom coming to earth in the person of Jesus Christ, to love and embrace the poor, the downcast, the brokenhearted, and the oppressed. Of course, the invitation for a relationship with God is open to anyone, but Jesus made it a special priority to address the hurting people in his midst, the sick in need of healing, and the impoverished. His church should do the same. "Come, follow me," he says, "and I will make you fishers of men."[1] But we can be fishers of men only if we are preaching a pure gospel.

"Be very careful. Keep a sharp eye out for the contaminating yeast of Pharisees and the followers of Herod."[2] According to Jesus, the gospel can be contaminated by at least two common attitudes, which can spread throughout the church and ruin the whole batch of dough. Some of the Pharisees were judgmental and hypocritical. Their religious instruction was heavy on control and rules and legalism and hoop jumping, and had a convenient way of overlooking the log in its own eye while barring entrance to God's kingdom for others. For example, a gospel contaminated by such a yeast might condemn a gay, married, and monogamous person for sexual immorality, while simultaneously saluting a twice-divorced, thrice-married, unrepentant serial adulterer and sexual assailant who sleeps with porn stars while his wife is home tending to their infant son. This is the type of hypocrisy Jesus can't stand.

The other contamination Jesus warns of is the yeast of Herod, which is political yeast. The followers of Herod are desperate for the type of power only a king can bequeath. Herod whispers, "Come follow me, and I will make you . . . as powerful as I am." It's a seductive offer, all right, but

1. Matt 4:19.
2. Mark 8:15.

it's a trap. Jesus never promised his followers that we would be politically powerful on earth. There is no reason for us to be. A fisher of men cannot also be a fisher of power.

The true and pure gospel, when it is uncontaminated by a religious or political mindset, empowers Christ followers to deeply love the world, and to humbly serve in it. Those are the only ideologies we need in order to bring heaven to earth and change the world. Religious legalism is not needed. Herod's power is not needed. Those influences both involve trying to force people into conformance with our religious and political ideologies. We don't need political power to preach a pure gospel. We need spiritual power. And what the church "gains" in political power via an alliance with a bully like Herod, it will lose in spiritual power. Allyship with Herod may make us feel special for a time in that we think we've achieved a political win—but according to Christ, a gospel contaminated by Herod is not a win for the actual kingdom of God at all.

* * *

For so many years, I made it my aim to "sell" my siblings on Jesus and the church. They were good sports about it. They came to my kids' various plays and programs, attended a few social functions at our Christian school, and came to hear me speak a few times. They were vaguely supportive, but aloof enough to let me know they weren't really interested. I talked up my most engaging Christian friends and made a concerted effort to introduce them to my sisters, to show them how fun and "normal" Christians could be. I just wanted them to experience the loving community of believers that Steve and I enjoyed.

But when Trumpism happened, a shift occurred. Some of the church started to sound less like Jesus and more like Herod, I mean, Trump. It was almost as if his narcissistic spirit had filtered down from the White House and landed on whomever was listening. Proverbs 18 says the tongue holds the power of life and death, and those that love it eat its fruit. Unfortunately, it seemed as though many in the church loved the toxic rhetoric coming out of their king's mouth, because they ate it and regurgitated it. Just like King Jeroboam, who held influence over Israel and "caused them to sin,"[3] Trump's most ardent supporters mimicked his overall attitude on a variety of issues. It was the contamination of

---

3. 1 Kgs 14:16.

Herod. "It's what comes out of a person that pollutes: obscenities, lusts, thefts, murders, adulteries, greed, depravity, deceptive dealings, carousing, mean looks, slander, arrogance, foolishness—all these are vomit from the heart. *There* is the source of your pollution."[4]

I started feeling less comfortable around some of my churchgoing friends. I flinched at their jokes about "owning the libs," "libtards," and voting out "feminists." Some of them referred to mask wearers as "mindless sheep." I noted the hypocrisy of buying bigger safes for all the guns they owned but refusing to wear a mask because "God would protect them." My brother Kevin, who at the time was the general manager of a Costco near Atlanta, Georgia, was forced to have to placate belligerent customers who refused to cooperate with store guidelines, in an effort to protect his customers and his own employees. It created such an unnecessary hardship for Kevin and for his employees, who were already working overtime in stressful conditions. Without a hint of irony, some Christians railed against the loss of their "personal rights" in having to wear a mask at the grocery store while forgetting that Jesus was all about protecting and caring for "the least of these," the most susceptible and vulnerable among us. They were sounding less like Christ and more like Trump all the time. Those same friends blew off stories of racism and oppression, claiming it was overblown—and of course the Trump-supporting political commentators they listened to had the statistics to prove it.

I read somewhere that you will emulate the five people you spend the most time with. If that's true, it explains the phenomenon of the spirit of Trumpism (the yeast of Herod) overtaking the spirit of Christ in the church. It's what happens when a vast majority of Christians are being discipled by media outlets, instead of by Jesus himself. I searched for a biblical explanation and I found it. "I can't believe your fickleness—how easily you have turned traitor to him who called you by the grace of Christ by embracing a variant message! It is not a minor variation, you know; it is completely other, an alien message, a no-message, a lie about God. Those who are provoking this agitation among you are turning the Message of Christ on its head."[5] Through the airwaves of extremist conservative media, the same outlets Trump himself promoted, the message of Christ had been turned on its head by the embrace of a variant gospel. This variant gospel sounded a heck of a lot more like Trump than it did the Jesus of the Gospels. It sounded

---

4. Mark 7:20–23.
5. Gal 1:6.

like a toxic blend of arrogance, hypocrisy, power lust, and narcissism, with a knack for belittling others thrown in for good measure. I believe Jesus would instruct his disciples to steer clear of it.

Commentators who get paid for appealing specifically to Christians are not necessarily following the Spirit of Christ. Many are just following the money. Christopher Hutchinson, the author of *Rediscovering Humility: Why the Way Up Is Down*, and the senior pastor of Grace Covenant Presbyterian Church in Blacksburg, Virginia, writes, "Christians should take their marching orders from Scripture. Not from talk radio which darkly speculates about a deep state conspiracy, and whose profit depends upon their audience's anger toward civil servants and other so-called 'elites.' Of all people, Christians should be ones who lead lives of quiet contentment rather than give into the resentment that fuels this sort of anti-establishment suspicion."[6]

A Christian should never align so closely with either political party that the commentary formulated for that one party is the only one they'll believe. When Fox News finally refused to air the president's ongoing lie that the 2020 election was "rigged and stolen," some of his followers just went further and further right until they found a source that *would* say what their itching ears wanted to hear. Trump knew this, and he capitalized on it, steering them toward propaganda outlets developed specifically to cater to his supporters.[7] A Christian who aims to represent the kingdom of God, not the kingdom of Republicans or the kingdom of Democrats, will let the Holy Spirit guide them to factual truth, not the "truth" as reported by their preferred source or party. If we spend our lives listening to fearmongering agitators, we will find ourselves becoming constantly offended, constantly angry, and constantly cynical. We will find ourselves treating people with contempt. This is a far cry from imitating Christ.

The kingdom of God is built on love. It is not built on political attainment. And we don't change the culture by going to war with it. We change the culture by serving it. While some of my churchgoing friends were calling mask wearers "misinformed idiots," and refusing to comply with safety measures designed to decrease the rate of the COVID-19 outbreak, my unchurched siblings were quietly considering the elderly and

---

6. Christopher A. Hutchinson, in Sider, *Spiritual Danger*, 205.

7. Donald J. Trump (@realDonaldTrump), "Watching @FoxNews is almost as bad as watching Fake News @CNN. New alternatives are developing!," Twitter, December 30, 2020, 1:27 p.m., https://twitter.com/realDonaldTrump/status/1344394741031514115.

the susceptible. While some of my churched friends were discounting racism and saying it wasn't real, my siblings were teaching their children to stand alongside communities of color. While some of my churched friends were waving flags around and touting Trump's "patriotism," my sisters, daughters of a real-life American war hero, were doing what every true patriot should have done: rebuking the president for slandering war heroes and Gold Star veterans. While my churched friends were justifying the separation of families at the border, my sisters were sending money to organizations that were hiring lawyers on the kids' behalf. While my churched friends were complaining about a perceived "infringement" on their own rights, my sisters were wearing masks without complaint, loving their neighbor ahead of themselves. They were simply following the Golden Rule, which my mom had taught us when we were young: "Do unto others as you would have them do unto you." So why would I want to invite my siblings to church? So that they could be contaminated by the yeast of Herod, aka Trumpism? No, thanks. In my view, they were already acting more Christlike than many in the church.

"I'm Here to Invite Outsiders, Not Coddle Insiders"[8]

Like the pollution caused by my scorched pizza, particles of contamination are sometimes difficult to discern—the particulates are so tiny that they are noticeable only in the narrow sunbeam where the light is flooding in. We can breathe in the air of a polluted gospel for so long we don't realize it. But Jesus's own proclamation will always recalibrate us to the good news, and who it is for:

> The Spirit of the Lord is on me,
>   because he has anointed me
>   to proclaim good news to the poor.
> He has sent me to proclaim freedom for the prisoners
>   and recovery of sight for the blind,
> to set the oppressed free,
>   to proclaim the year of the Lord's favor.[9]

---

8. Jesus, Matt 9:13.
9. Luke 4:18–19 NET.

If our stance on an issue is determined mostly by "this is what's best for me," but it isn't good news to the poor, or the sick or immunocompromised, or the elderly, or the person without health care, it's not a Christ-filled stance. Jesus is hope for the poverty stricken. He is hope for the immigrant, the refugee, the displaced, and the homeless. Jesus is hope for the marginalized, the abused, the depressed, the abandoned, and the brokenhearted among us. So whatever we are preaching, it had better be good news to their ears, or it's not the gospel of Jesus Christ. A pure gospel puts other people first. A pure gospel doesn't overly concern itself with its own "rights." A pure gospel relies on spiritual power, not Herod's power, to change the world. A pure gospel cares more for the least of these than it does for itself, and does not stain itself with worldly quests for political gain that, in the end, will do nothing to prosper the kingdom of God. Power is as seductive as hell. It's tempting to exchange the pure gospel for one that garners political control. But Herod's yeast is contaminated, and it spreads quickly throughout the whole batch of dough. Keep a sharp eye out for the followers of Herod, lest we become one.

12

Human Scum

> Let me tell you something: Every one of these careless words is going to come back to haunt you. There will be a time of Reckoning. Words are powerful; take them seriously. Words can be your salvation. Words can also be your damnation.—Matt 12:34–37

Three years into Trump's presidency, you would think I'd have become accustomed to his strange and abusive tweets, but they continued to rattle me. I was hoping that those who were on his evangelical ministry council were correct in their assertion that despite mounting evidence to the contrary, Trump was being used by God. But God does not "use" people who deliberately choose meanness and wickedness, time and time again.[1] So either the council was thoroughly deceived or deliberately gaslighting me. Trump's personal messages via tweet to the citizens of America told the true story of what was in his heart.[2] He sometimes shot them off in rapid succession in the wee hours of the morning, giving targets of his vitriol something extra special to wake up to. Like this one, in October 2019: "The Never Trumper Republicans, though on respirators with not many left, are in certain ways worse and more dangerous for our Country than the Do Nothing Democrats. Watch out for them, they are human scum!"[3]

1. Gal 6:7–8; Hos 9:15.
2. Luke 6:45.
3. Donald J. Trump (@realDonaldTrump), "The Never Trumper Republicans," Twitter,

THE JUDAS EFFECT

I choked and accidentally sprayed coffee all over my phone. Surely, he could not be serious. This one *had* to be from a parody account. But news reports confirmed it was actually from the acting president of the United States. I felt sick, as if I had been personally attacked by POTUS. I had the same feeling in the pit of my stomach that I had had in fifth grade with the bus bully. There had been so many inane tweets, but I realized this one felt most jarring because he was talking about *me*. I had voted Republican my entire adult life, but I would never vote for Donald Trump. According to him, that made me not only vile and worthless, but a bad patriot. I couldn't honestly decide which felt like the worst insult.

I reflected on my childhood as the daughter of a war hero. My mom had married Captain James R. Shively when I was five years old. He was relatively well known in our hometown of Spokane, Washington, and people treated him like a mini-celebrity of sorts. When we went into a grocery store or restaurant, people often recognized him and came up to shake his hand. I quickly learned that my dad was a hero, and as his new daughter, a certain pride in America was instilled in my young heart. I was a rather excited patriot, even for such a small child. My favorite puzzle was of the United States, with thick, brightly colored wooden chunks representing each state. By the time I was eight years old, I had memorized all the states in alphabetical order, along with their capital cities. My dad and I played a game that began when we went to a restaurant that had a blank map of the United States as the children's place mat. We raced each other to fill in the names of the states, and then we had another race to fill in the state capitals. After that, every time we went to a restaurant, I brought paper so that if they didn't have a children's place mat you could draw on, Dad and I could still play the states game.

I love America. I love everything about it. I love the shape of it. I love the north, south, east, and west, the different dialects, the redwoods, the mountain ranges, the coasts, the islands, everything. I love that it is your land, and it is my land, the land of the free and the home of the brave. In the fourth grade I learned to sing the names of all the presidents, in order, to the tune of "Yankee Doodle Dandy." I can sing it to this day, and I do, as my husband thinks it's hilarious to put me on the spot at parties. (Of course I've had to add a few names, since when I learned it, the song ended with Reagan.)

October 23, 2019, 10:48 a.m., https://twitter.com/realDonaldTrump/status/1187063301731209220.

HUMAN SCUM

Steve and I consider ourselves to be strong American patriots. We have a flag waving in front of our home, in tribute to our country and her protectors. I wrote a book about Vietnam prisoners of war, not only to honor my dad and the men he fought beside, but to inspire my kids' generation, so they would know and understand the sacrifices that have been made for their security and freedom.

I want the very best for our country. I want us to be safe and united and strong, and I want us to care about each other enough to argue about things that matter. There is room in our political discourse for disagreement on policies. What there isn't room for is name-calling and abuse.

"Human scum" is a phrase borrowed straight out of Hitler's playbook. It worked well for Hitler, as a tactic of dehumanizing his enemies, and unfortunately it seemed to also work well for Donald. The phrase was quickly picked up and recirculated all over social media by those who loved to spread his poison, and was even defended by his White House press secretary.

Meanwhile, Trump pretended to be the consummate American patriot while dodging the draft, mocking war heroes and their families, calling American soldiers "losers" and "suckers," soliciting foreign leaders to interfere in our elections, bragging about avoiding taxes, taking health care from families, using taxpayer money to fund his campaign and then rerouting the money to his own companies, circulating Russian propaganda, citing Vladimir Putin as someone to be admired, pretending a free and fair election was "stolen," and inciting violence at the Capitol.[4] These are things a nationalist who wants to rule by any means necessary would do. They are not something a true patriot who had America's best interests at heart would do.[5]

Donald's governing strategy was clear, Making America Great Again by insulting her citizens and pitting them against each other one abusive tweet at a time. But what pained me even more was the relative silence of his ministry council, who refused to publicly rebuke him. It made me wonder if they were actually scared of Donald Trump, because they sure weren't scared of God. "Whoever whitewashes the wicked gets a black

---

4. Timothy Snyder, *On Tyranny: Twenty Lessons from the Twentieth Century* (New York: Random House, 2017), 112–13.

5. See Snyder, *On Tyranny*, 113–14, for the differences between a patriot and a nationalist.

mark in the history books, / But whoever exposes the wicked will be thanked and rewarded."⁶

The wickedness in this man's heart had been laid bare on more than one occasion for all the world to see. With such a notable lack of rebuke from evangelical leaders, I was left to wonder if pro-Trump Christians agreed with him that I, and millions of others who refused to jump on the Trump bandwagon, were simply unworthy of human dignity. Did Trump and his evangelical supporters hope that I would crawl on the floor and eat worms for the rest of my days, unless I agreed to change my mind and vote for him?

I'll probably never know the answers to my questions but I do know this: any leader in the church who refused to condemn Trump's degrading words is no leader at all. And if refusing to vote for a mean-spirited, divisive, abusive bully makes me what he says I am, I shall gladly remain, yours truly, forever and always, Human Scum.

"Mean-tempered leaders are like mad dogs."⁷

---

6. Prov 24:24.
7. Prov 19:12.

13

The Power of Life and Death

Death and life are in the power of the tongue, and those who love it will eat its fruit.—Prov 18:21 NET

While working as a teacher's aide at my kids' Christian elementary school, I once sent a third-grader to the principal's office for calling his classmate a "facebutt." (I think he got the phrasing a little wrong, but his listener had no problem understanding the overall sentiment.) He had to miss recess. I felt bad; he was such a cutie and I knew he needed recess to get his wiggles out, but he also needed to learn that his words held consequences. It's better to learn that lesson when you are eight than when you are seventy-eight.

Throughout his term, our former president's words largely went unsanctioned by those in a position to hold him accountable. Our country paid a tragic price for this neglect on January 6, 2021.

The power of life and death is in the tongue, and that is never more true than when the person speaking is in a position of high authority. Standing on a raised platform, in front of a crowd of followers invited by him,[1] Donald Trump's words created an atmosphere dripping with violence. As discussed in previous chapters, this was nothing new. His campaign rallies often turned into cesspools of anger and chaos, with

---

1. Donald J. Trump (@realDonaldTrump), "Big protest in DC on January 6th. Be there, will be wild!," Twitter, December 19, 2020, 1:42 a.m., https://www.presidency.ucsb.edu/documents/tweets-december-19-2020.

attendees screaming insults, using misogynistic and racist phrasing, bullying the press, and even punching protestors as Trump himself egged them on. In Cleveland, one Trump supporter told a Black woman to "go back to Africa," while another screamed, "Go back to Auschwitz." Rather than condemn the hateful rhetoric so prevalent at his rallies, Trump called his supporters "spirited" and spoke from the stage about how he would like to punch a protester in the mouth.[2]

In some cases, Trump himself spoke the hateful words, and, as Prov 18:21 suggests, those who loved his words "ate" them and regurgitated them back. You may even say his tongue held sway over them.

> For five years Trump publicly pushed the ridiculous, racist lie that Barack Obama was born in Kenya. Although disproved, what did Trump's followers continue to chant at his rallies?
> "Obama is Muslim!"[3]
>
> From his platform, Trump demonized (brown and Black) immigrants, insisting that they are "infectious" murderers and rapists from "shithole countries" who want to take away jobs.
> His followers scream: "Immigrants need to get the hell out!"[4]
>
> Up on stage, Trump let the insults fly. He referred to Mitt Romney as a "choke artist," Hillary Clinton, "Crooked Hillary," and Elizabeth Warren, "Pocahontas." The crowd's reply: "She's a C%#t, Vote Trump!"[5] and, "Assassinate that b$tch."[6]
>
> Trump regularly and systematically told his followers that the press is "fake," "third-rate," "awful," "disgraceful," "the enemy of the people." And his followers responded at his rallies: "F#@k you, media!"[7]

Every time the press covered a Trump rally, they witnessed a foreshadowing of the events of January 6. They saw firsthand how the crowds responded to his angry rhetoric. It's no wonder some were forced to hire bodyguards, just for telling the truth. It's no wonder some of them regularly

---

2. Tur, *Unbelievable*, 176.
3. Tur, *Unbelievable*, 244.
4. Tur, *Unbelievable*, 244.
5. Tur, *Unbelievable*, 178, 244–45.
6. Tur, *Unbelievable*, 276.
7. Tur, *Unbelievable*, 244.

received death threats.[8] They knew that someday Donald Trump's more fanatic followers would make good on Donald's not-so-subtle threats. And Donald knew it too. He knew his words have power, he practiced using them on large crowds for several years. He was banking on it.

January 6, 2021

Although he lost by more than seven million votes,[9] Trump spent weeks whipping his followers up into a frenzy with false allegations of election fraud. Never mind that both state and federal courts had thrown out nearly four dozen Trump lawsuits attempting to upend the results.

"Big protest in DC on January 6th. Be there, will be wild!" Trump had promised them.[10] And it was. At his behest, a crowd of thousands gathered to join their leader in protest of the election results. Their protest included smashing windows, spreading feces and urine in the corridors of the Capitol building, destroying statues and other historical relics, threatening to hang Mike Pence (for telling the truth by certifying the election results), and killing five people while injuring hundreds more. Trump stood at the Ellipse, behind the White House, and delivered the speech that earned him a second impeachment, this time for "incitement of insurrection." It was the most bipartisan presidential impeachment in history and also the first presidential impeachment in which all majority caucus members voted unanimously. His rhetoric led to swift rebuke from members of his own party.

A statement by Senator Mitt Romney read,

> We gather today due to a selfish man's injured pride and the outrage of his supporters whom he has deliberately misinformed for the past two months and stirred to action this very morning. What happened here today was an insurrection, incited by the President of the United States. Those who choose to continue to support his dangerous gambit by objecting to the results of a legitimate, democratic election will forever be seen as being

---

8. Tina Nguyen, "Donald Trump Hates Journalists but Says He Won't Kill Them; We Feel Much Safer Already," *Vanity Fair*, December 12, 2015, https://www.vanityfair.com/news/2015/12/trump-wont-kill-journalists.

9. "Presidential Election Results: Biden Wins," *New York Times*, Nov. 3, 2020, https://www.nytimes.com/interactive/2020/11/03/us/elections/results-president.html.

10. Donald J. Trump (@realDonaldTrump), Twitter, December 19, 2020, 1:42 a.m., https://www.presidency.ucsb.edu/documents/tweets-december-19-2020.

complicit in an unprecedented attack against our democracy. They will be remembered for their role in this shameful episode in American history. That will be their legacy.[11]

Liz Cheney stated,

> The President of the United States summoned this mob, assembled the mob, and lit the flame of this attack. Everything that followed was his doing. None of this would have happened without the President. There has never been a greater betrayal by a President of the United States of his office and his oath to the Constitution.[12]

From General James Mattis,

> Today's violent assault on our Capitol, an effort to subjugate American democracy by mob rule, was fomented by Mr. Trump.[13]

General Colin Powell went so far as to renounce his own party, stating that Republican officials "should have known better" than to support Mr. Trump, but they were so taken by their political standing, "none of them wanted to put themselves at political risk" by speaking out against him. "We need people that will speak the truth," he admonished.[14] I tend to think Jesus would agree.

Even Mitch McConnell placed the blame squarely where it belonged:

> The mob was fed lies. . . . They were provoked by the president and other powerful people, and they tried to use fear and violence to stop a specific proceeding of the first branch of the federal government, which they did not like.[15]

---

11. Mitt Romney, "Romney Condemns Insurrection at U.S. Capitol," Mitt Romney, January 6, 2021, para. 2, https://www.romney.senate.gov/romney-condemns-insurrection-us-capitol.

12. Liz Cheney, *Oath and Honor: A Memoir and a Warning* (New York: Little, Brown, 2023), 137.

13. Steve Holland et al., "Trump Summoned Supporters to 'Wild' Protest, and Told Them to Fight. They Did," *Reuters*, January 7, 2021, para. 24, https://www.reuters.com/article/us-usa-election-protests/trump-summoned-supporters-to-wild-protest-and-told-them-to-fight-they-did-idUSKBN29B24S.

14. Azi Paybarah, "Colin Powell Says He 'Can No Longer Call Himself a Republican,'" *New York Times*, January 11, 2021, para. 7, https://www.nytimes.com/2021/10/18/us/colin-powell-gop.html.

15. Kelsey Snell and Barbara Sprunt, "'The Mob Was Fed Lies': McConnell Rebukes Trump for His Role in Capitol Riot," NPR, January 19, 2021, paras. 2–3, https://www.npr.org/sections/insurrection-at-the-capitol/2021/01/19/958410118/this-mob-was-fed-lies-mcconnell-rebukes-trump-for-his-role-in-capitol-riot.

Three White House aides, including McConnell's wife Elaine Chao, immediately resigned.

Jesus's brother James invites us to consider the source of such extreme, unnecessary violence.

> Where do you think all these appalling wars and quarrels come from? Do you think they just happen? Think again. They come about because you want your own way, and fight for it deep inside yourselves. You lust for what you don't have and are willing to kill to get it. You want what isn't yours and will risk violence to get your hands on it.[16]

When I heard about the assault on our Capitol, I left work and went home to turn on the news, as nauseous as it made me. I had been to Washington, DC, just three years prior, to speak at the National Archives about the Vietnam prisoner of war experience and to conduct a book signing for *Six Years in the Hanoi Hilton*. My entire DC experience was thrilling, but nothing captivated my imagination more than the glorious rotunda in the Capitol building. I couldn't help but spin a few circles under the magnificent domed ceiling, under the watchful eyes of the statues of Presidents Reagan, Truman, and Jefferson. I found out later that the statues I so admired had sustained chemical damage, the house floor was defecated on, historic murals were damaged, and technical equipment was broken and/or stolen. The building sustained upwards of $30 million in damages.[17] This desecration of a national landmark happened for one reason and one reason only: because one man couldn't stand that he lost an election, and he wielded his tongue to call for violence on his behalf.

Exactly as they had at his rallies, the mob parroted his words back to him. "*Fight for Trump!*" they screamed, while waving a motley assortment of American, Confederate, Trump, and Christian flags. I was incredulous. "Who on earth would really believe this man enough to do this?" I asked my husband. But the live footage on our TV screen answered my question. Those four flags waving together told me everything I needed to know. Nazis, the Proud Boys, "patriots," and professing Christians, all marching together at the direction of the man for whom they shared a mutual esteem. I learned later that as the Senate evacuated, and Mike

---

16. Jas 4:1–2.

17. Bill Chappell, "Architect of the Capitol Outlines $30 Million in Damages from Pro-Trump Riot," NPR, February 24, 2021, https://www.npr.org/sections/insurrection-at-the-capitol/2021/02/24/970977612/architect-of-the-capitol-outlines-30-million-in-damages-from-pro-trump-riot.

Pence ran for cover, high-ranking members of Congress representing both parties called the president and begged him to call off the mob. They were ignored. For three long hours, during which five people died, 140 police officers were injured, and $30 million in damages was sustained, he refused. When a person is overtaken by a lust for power, he will do anything to obtain it. Anything for the "win."

"Anything for the Win"

It's a motto of Trump's that seems to have been adopted by many Christ followers who even today attempt to keep up the ruse. It's not difficult for anyone with a fourth grade education to see, simply by watching the video of his speech, and by reading the transcript of his words, that Trump incited the violence on January 6. By insisting on his innocence, some Christians have revealed a lust for power, accompanied by denial, which is greater than their desire for truth. They have chosen instead to defend a man who is loud enough, violent enough, and seductive enough to give them the political power they really, really want.

> They are loudmouths, full of hot air, but still they're dangerous. Men and women who have recently escaped from a deviant life are most susceptible to their brand of seduction. They promise these newcomers freedom, but they themselves are slaves of corruption, for if they're addicted to corruption—and they are— they're *enslaved*.[18]

"Fight like hell!" Donald Trump had commanded them. "You will never take back our country with weakness!" "Show strength!" "If you don't fight like hell you're not going to have a country anymore," "Go by very different rules!" "Fight to the death. . . . I'll be with you,"[19] he promised them (before heading back inside the White House to watch it all on television).

An Unholy Spiritual Alliance

My favorite part of any church service is communion. To me, it is the highest, most holy act in a believer's life, as it signifies our spiritual union

---

18. 2 Pet 2:17–19; emphasis original.

19. Associated Press, "Transcript of Trump's Speech at Rally before US Capitol Riot," *U.S. News*, January 13, 2021, https://www.usnews.com/news/politics/articles/2021-01-13/transcript-of-trumps-speech-at-rally-before-us-capitol-riot.

with God. Our Father sets a table before his children, and invites us to eat the bread of life and drink from the cup of his blessing. We take communion to remember that we are partakers of the Lord, and we are united as one with him. This demonstration of sacred partnership reminds us that we will spend an eternity with him, and it is also meant to empower us to share his love and goodness with the rest of the world. Communion strengthens us inwardly so we can love our neighbors as ourselves, lend compassion and grace and resources to those in need, rescue the perishing, extend hope, and stand with the oppressed.

The enemy wants a spiritual alliance with us too. This is why, when discussing taking communion, the apostle Paul warns us to be aware of feasting with idols.[20] The enemy's idea of a joint partnership involves unleashing hatred, chaos, and violence onto the world, instead of love and blessing. As God offers bread and wine as symbols for our spiritual sustenance, so too does the enemy dangle out tasty bait in hopes we will take a bite. His offer of an apple worked on Eve, of course. It also worked on Judas Iscariot; the enemy entered Judas when he took a bite of bread at the Last Supper. But Jesus was not so easily tempted. He knew better than to turn the stones into bread. And the prophet Daniel refused to consume what King Nebuchadnezzar was dishing out. Some offerings, no matter how hungry we are, or how delicious they look, are just not fit for consumption. Eve learned the hard way that not every piece of fruit is worth the bite. One must discern when it is the serpent doing the offering.

Trump's offering to his followers is disunity, bedlam, sexism, racism, violence, and abuse. He just serves up his words on a rich, gold-plated platter, and covers them in "Christianese," so that followers of Christ will take a bite. Ask yourself this: Why would Christians align themselves with someone who pretended not to know who David Duke was?[21] Because the fruit of racism is easier to swallow when it's coated in a hyper-patriotic red-white-and-blue marmalade. Why would Christians support a person who mocks a prisoner of war and insults a Gold Star family? Because Trump covered his foul offering with a thick layer of "I'll give you a Supreme Court justice" sauce. Why would Christians maintain an affiliation with a man who calls a woman a "low I.Q., crazy, bimbo"? Because misogyny goes down smooth with a glass of "Merry Christmas." Why would Christians continue to defend someone whose words led a violent, angry,

20. 1 Cor 10:14–22.
21. Domonoske, "Trump Fails to Condemn."

riotous mob to desecrate our nation's Capitol? Because political power is a sumptuous ten-course banquet we will sell our souls for.

Some Evangelicals feasted richly at Donald Trump's table, but it was a dinner party from hell, catered by the devil himself. Not only did the Trump buffet poison the church, but the very world we are supposed to be reaching for Christ doesn't want anything to do with us now. And they are right to turn their noses up at our stinking plate of hypocrisy. God doesn't like it either. The alliance with Donald Trump not only cost us our witness, it impugned the very nature and character of God.

> I don't want you to become part of something that reduces you to less than yourself. And you can't have it both ways, banqueting with the Master one day and slumming with demons the next. Besides, the Master won't put up with it.[22]

We can't feast with God and snack on what the devil is serving at the same time. It is impossible. By offering us political power, and soaking up our approval, our praise, and in some cases, our downright obedience in return, the enemy forged a union. This alliance with darkness was made crystal clear in the events of January 6. When Donald Trump served up the words "meet me at the Capitol" . . . "it'll be wild" . . . "fight" . . . "show strength!" . . . "You will never take our country back with weakness" . . . "go by very different rules!" . . . "I'll be with you!," the power of death and violence was on his tongue. He knew exactly what he was offering to his disciples. He was offering them power, if only they would obey him. And those who loved his words ate them.

---

22. 1 Cor 10:20–21.

14

Welcome to Adventureland

> God, who got you started in this spiritual adventure, shares with us the life of his Son and our Master Jesus. He will never give up on you. Never forget that.—1 Cor 1:7–9

I was gloriously naive, coming into the church in 1999. The brightly colored sign in our children's ministry hallway said, "Welcome to Adventureland," and that's exactly how I felt. Every day was a new adventure. I remember the first time I noticed the ark cutout on the wall of the nursery, with the little animals lined up two by two marching into it, and a Scripture verse underneath. It dawned on me what I was looking at. "You mean Noah's ark is in the *Bible*?," I exclaimed, to the utter delight of the volunteer working that day. Who would have guessed that? I'd always thought Noah's ark was from Mother Goose or something. I was in my mid-twenties, a new mom, and I felt like a kid in a foreign land, strolling the hallways of the church with a baby in my arms and a toddler hanging from my leg, opening doors of mystery I had never even known existed. I had so much to learn, and between my new Bible study community, church services twice a week, discipleship class, ministry involvement, and various planning committees, I was there nearly every day. I was a willing, eager student, with an endless list of questions. My pastors, mentors, and Bible study leaders fed me a steady milk diet of Scripture, until, like the writer of Hebrews suggests, I graduated to solid food.

Steve, the social guy that he is, was happy as a clam too. We were loaded up with friends and activities. We knew we belonged. It was such an endearing time for us. I'm sure we look back with rose-colored glasses, but it truly seems like those days held a special charm. We were new parents, new Christians, and we were grateful even then for so many friends and the mentors who encouraged us along the way. There was always a gathering, and we hated to miss it, and in fact, we'd hear about it later if we did. We learned quickly that people keep tabs on you when you are part of a church. So we toted our little children around to potlucks and fellowship parties and pastor-appreciation banquets. The pace was slightly frenetic, which partially accounts for the abrupt shock we felt when we left.

Fast-forward twenty years. The (mostly white) evangelical embrace of Donald Trump told us where we *didn't* belong, but now we had no idea where we *did* belong. Prior to our departure, we'd never even considered that there was another way to "do" Christianity outside of white, American-style Evangelicalism. After we left our evangelical bubble, I pictured us wandering through the wilderness with Jesus, searching for a new bubble to break into. We bounced around from worship community to worship community, hoping to find a good fit.

Every church we visited proclaimed Christ, but they all had their own way of representing Christ, and sometimes those representations differed greatly. The denomination we had come out of was big on missions; it was also big on guns (2A rights!), wealth (it was OK to drive a Porsche or a Corvette, as long as you tithed regularly), and patriotism, with a giant American flag that flew wildly outside the front door, sometimes positioned on top of the Christian flag.

The contrast to our next faith community was startling. The Anabaptists shunned guns completely, as violent weapons of war utterly abhorrent to our peace-loving God. Flashy displays of wealth were against the ways of Christ altogether. The American flag was considered an idol, because why would you pledge allegiance to anything or anyone other than Christ? Our time with the Anabaptists was quiet and simple, with small meetings that felt like a balm to our souls in a chaotic time. They explained that a follower of Christ lives simply, so that others may simply live. That meant growing a lot of your own food and not wasting anything. (When the Anabaptists came over, I felt guilty for watering my lawn.)

The Pentecostal church was fun. Charismatics were big on Holy Spirit power. If you didn't have it, you weren't accurately representing Christ. "A gospel without power is not the gospel Jesus preached," our Pentecostal pastor told us. He went on to explain, "The Holy Spirit's power is available to you. He is always pouring out the wine. You can bring a cup, a carafe, or a large bucket, it's up to you." Worship was energetic, lively, and loud. It was even entertaining; they had dancers who waved flags in time with the music, and artists that painted onstage.

There was a Missionary Baptist church in our small town, but we discovered this particular one was semi-famous for putting up a bigoted, anti-Islamic message on the reader board. We labeled it the "mean" church and didn't bother to visit. We also had a perfectly lovely Mennonite community nearby, but I had already ruled it out on the grounds that my hair doesn't look good long.

Then I remembered I was a confirmed Episcopalian. I hadn't set foot in an Episcopal church since our wedding day. The hymns and rituals, which I would have found boring at any other point in my spiritual journey, were strangely comforting. We discovered that Episcopalians let women preach. The presiding bishop over the entire denomination, Bishop Michael Curry, had delivered a sermon at Prince Harry and Meghan's wedding ceremony. His touching soliloquy heard around the world had seemed to refute Trumpism. This one was looking better all the time.

Steve and I considered our options. We had fit in well when we were "baby Christians," back in the glory days of Adventureland, being spoon-fed mashed-up doctrine that we could easily digest. But now that we'd graduated to solid food, we were out on our own in the cold, harsh wilderness, and we didn't seem to really fit anywhere. We were too progressive for some conservatives and too conservative for some progressives. We could guzzle Holy Spirit wine with the Pentecostals, partake of our daily bread with the Christian Missionary Alliance, live simply on homegrown food with the Anabaptists, or enjoy quiet communion with the Episcopalians. Or, we could stay in the wilderness with Jesus and do church online, which I likened to John the Baptist's lonely diet of locusts and honey. I knew internet church wouldn't sustain us for long. We needed the people. But who were our people? We were finding there were so many ways to be a Christian in the world. Who was doing it "right"?

* * *

So much of the Christian life is about trying to "get it right." We want to please God, please our pastor, please our Christian friends. Can we drink?

Can we smoke? Can women teach, and if so, exactly to whom and for how long? Can gay people come? If so, can they have leadership roles? Should babies be baptized? Sprinkle or dunk? Is it okay to call God a woman, since there are several verses that liken God to a Mother in Scripture? Or is that considered blasphemous? *What about the Earth?* Are we into climate change, Y/N? Can I do the Enneagram, or will it send me on a downward spiral into the New Age abyss from which Jesus will never be able to save me? What about yoga, for that matter? How do we feel about the spiritual gifts, speaking in tongues, praying for miracles and healings, giving prophetic words, is this okay, Y/N?

Here's what I decided. After twenty years of trying, there is no "getting it right." Wherever I land on any certain issue, it's going to rile someone up. Maybe the best way to approach Christianity is to embrace your own adventure with Jesus and let other people have theirs. It's Adventureland from the moment you decide to follow Christ until the day he takes you home. It takes a certain degree of humility to admit this. It takes a certain degree of humility to realize that, try as we may, our own Christian bubble is probably not getting everything right. There may actually be another representation of Christ that is more accurate than the one we ourselves have been living. And that's okay. Jesus saved you the first time, he'll come find you wherever you are. You can be stark raving mad on a hill in Gerasenes, alone in the wilderness, on the road to Damascus with just one other person, in a conservative community, in a progressive community, dancing with flags or sitting quietly in the hymnal. You can make your bed in the pit of hell. He'll find you there too. God designed it that way, because God loves an adventure, and he isn't as afraid of our mistakes as we are. We're not going to get it all right, anyway. There's freedom in the adventure. "He brought me out into a spacious place; he rescued me because he delighted in me" (Ps 18:19 NIV).

In the end, I went back to my Episcopalian "roots." Without shame, without fear, and without overexplaining my decision to anyone. There are roughly thirty-four thousand Christian denominations in the world,[1] and each one of them probably thinks they are the one that has it all right. But you know what? Only God knows.

And she's not telling.

---

1. Howard Kramer, "How Many Churches and Denominations Are There in the World?," Complete Pilgrim, May 30, 2022, https://thecompletepilgrim.com/many-churches-denominations-america-world/.

15

Choose Life

> It is a strange thing to live in a world where we can be pro-military, pro-guns, pro-executions, and still say we are pro-life so long as we stand against abortion.
> —Shane Claiborne[1]

Telling people I'm pro-life gives me a shot of adrenaline. I don't deny it. It makes me feel holy and, dare I say, just a tiny bit self-righteous, to be a protector of the innocents. I can lord my pro-life stance over anyone, anytime, throw it into any argument whether it's on topic or not, and walk away feeling like the winner. I, the pro-life person, can happily proclaim myself to be the superior being with the highest possible morals.

I didn't figure out, until 2016, that I was using my pro-life stance as my personal beacon of morality, without bothering to dig into other important issues that are also a matter of life and death. Like the number of refugees who will live or die based on our country's current policy. Or how many DACA recipients may be put in an unsafe, life-or-death situation if forced to leave the United States. Wearing a mask in the middle of a global pandemic is a pro-life issue. Either you care about other people's lives or you don't. Fighting for health care for people who need it, and for relief bills that will feed hungry children, and for commonsense gun laws, are pro-life

---

1. Shane Claiborne, *Rethinking Life: Embracing the Sacredness of Every Person* (Grand Rapids: Zondervan, 2023), 2.

issues too. I also had never bothered myself to learn that the abortion rate goes down during Democratic presidencies and rises during Republican presidencies, largely due to availability of health care and contraception.

If we want to talk about matters that God considers wicked, let's talk about abortion. But let's not stop there, because the Bible doesn't. We must then talk about passing bills that will benefit poor people instead of giving tax breaks to billionaires. Because according to God,

> The righteous care about justice for the poor,
> but the wicked have no such concern.[2]

After we have discussed abortion laws and concern for the poor, it's imperative that we talk about refugees, many of whom are faith-filled Christians. Listen to how the apostle John commends the church for their hospitality toward foreigners in need:

> Dear friend, when you extend hospitality to Christian brothers and sisters, even when they are strangers, you make the faith visible. They've made a full report back to the church here, a message about your love. It's good work you're doing, helping these travelers on their way, hospitality worthy of God himself! They set out under the banner of the Name, and get no help from unbelievers. So they deserve any support we can give them. In providing meals and a bed, we become their companions in spreading the Truth.[3]

Now compare it to how he chastises a leader who refuses to offer this same hospitality:

> Earlier I wrote something along this line to the church, but Diotrephes, who loves being in charge, denigrates my counsel. If I come, you can be sure I'll hold him to account for spreading vicious rumors about us. As if that weren't bad enough, he not only refuses hospitality to traveling Christians *but tries to stop others from welcoming them. Worse yet, instead of inviting them in he throws them out.* Friend, don't go along with evil. Model the good. The person who does good does God's work. The person who does evil falsifies God, doesn't know the first thing about God.[4]

If John calls Diotrephes' policies "evil," I wonder what he would have to say about Trump's policies, which separated over 5,500 families at the border,

2. Prov 29:7 NIV.
3. 3 John 1:5–8.
4. 3 John 1:9–11; emphasis added.

causing the precious children and their parents a lifetime of agony and psychological trauma. He put tens of thousands of asylum seekers and migrants in life-threatening danger, left the lives of 180,000 DACA dreamers hanging in the balance with threats of deportation, and violated United States refugee law by shutting the door on displaced persons.[5] The Trump administration's unprecedented immigration protocols biblically disqualified the United States from any pretense we ever had of being a "Christian" nation.

We are all image bearers of a great and marvelous God. This is true of the baby in the womb. It's true of the homeless. It's true of the poverty stricken. It's true of the Pakistani refugee and the Mexican immigrant at the southern border. Those who welcome the stranger welcome Jesus himself. Choosing life means voting for legislators that concern themselves with the poor. It means putting government officials in place who will show compassion to travelers in need. We can protect our borders and treat the sojourner with respect at the same time.

I no longer feel self-righteous when I say I'm pro-life. I just feel humbled, and somewhat ineffective, because I know in my heart of hearts I could do more to allow life to prosper around me. Biblically speaking, if my fervor for the first nine months of life isn't matched by equal fervor for protecting and advocating the years after, I'm not truly pro-life. I'm just pro-pregnancy.

---

5. Human Rights First, "Chaos, Cruelty, & Illegality: The Trump Administration's Record on Asylum," Human Rights First, January 12, 2021, https://humanrightsfirst.org/library/chaos-cruelty-illegality-the-trump-administrations-record-on-asylum/.

16

Leave Her Alone

Jesus said, "Leave her alone." —Mark 14:6

The religious leaders dragged a shamed, frightened, partially dressed woman through the streets of Jerusalem. When they found Jesus preaching at the temple, they thrust her out in front of the crowd and asked, "What should we do with her?" She had been caught in an adulterous affair. Lawfully, she should be stoned. Jesus knew the law full well, they just wanted to hear him say it.

The bullies stood in a circle around her with their fists raised and rocks ready, waiting for his answer. They expected Jesus to take their side. She was guilty, and it was the law. But he didn't. He was not about to let them hurt her. Standing up, he looked at each of them pointedly. "Let any one of you who is without sin throw the first stone at her."[1] One by one they dropped their stones, turned around, and walked away.

Later, at a party, a grateful woman approached Jesus and poured a year's supply of expensive oil on his feet, in a symbolic gesture of gratitude and love. Judas stood to scold her, but Jesus rebuked him before he got very far. "Leave her alone," Jesus told him. And so he sat back down and shut back up.

Just pause and reflect on those three little words for a moment. "Leave. Her. Alone." Strung together, they are three of the most beautiful words in all of Scripture. Try to imagine the scene. How happy she must

---

1. John 8:7 NIV.

have been to share her oil with the one she loved most. And how a gruff man, bigger in size, bigger in clout, tried to diminish her. But Jesus wasn't having it. He simply was not having it. Try to imagine the tone of Christ's voice when he said it: "Leave her alone." For women—those three words are a gorgeous revelation of Jesus's heart toward them. For men—they should be taken as a warning.

Men, you need to know this: Jesus is paying attention. Every time a woman (or a child) is bullied, he knows about it. Every time she is abused, he sees. Every time she is touched without her express permission, he's watching. Every time she is called a name, or belittled in any way, he's taking note. He knows. He knows. And if you think you are getting away with something, you aren't. There is no greater defender or protector of women than Jesus Christ. If you have mistreated a woman, and you have not repented both to the Lord and to her, I urge you to do it quickly. There absolutely will be a day of reckoning with Jesus, and I promise you this: you don't want that misconduct hanging over your head.

God does not forgive abuse that has not been repented of. In fact, I'm not sure there is anything that makes him angrier than one person misusing another. "But if you give them a hard time, bullying or taking advantage of their simple trust, you'll soon wish you hadn't. You'd be better off dropped in the middle of the lake with a millstone around your neck."[2] Every time and in every scriptural example, God sides with the ill-treated, the mishandled, and the bullied. And a church that is accurately representing God will be angry about bullying too.

Donald Trump's hatefulness toward women continued throughout his campaign and into his presidency, and went largely ignored by the evangelical church. Megyn Kelly was a "bimbo" who had "blood coming out of her wherever"; Rosie O'Donnell was assaulted as a "fat loser"; Carly Fiorina shouldn't get votes "because of her face"; Alicia Machado, "Miss Piggy"; columnist Gail Collins, "the face of a dog!"; Arianna Huffington, "extremely unattractive." Mika Brzezinski was deemed "low I.Q., crazy, bleeding badly from a face-lift." Carmen Yulin Cruz, the mayor of San Juan, desperate to get help on behalf of her suffering citizens, was accused of being "nasty," and wanting "everything done for (her)."

His abuse became so commonplace no one was shocked anymore. And really, why should any of us have been surprised that even from his high seat in the Oval Office, he was living by his own "you have to treat [women]

2. Matt 18:6.

like s---" mantra?³ No, what was shocking was the church's dismissal of it. When a man in a high position, elected largely by Evangelicals, spews forth hatred and abuse toward women: that spirit of bullying gains momentum. Unchecked and uncorrected, the abuse gains force and multiplies. A church that is not actively, vocally speaking out against lewd and aggressive behavior toward women, is partnering with it. And our silence could not be a more erroneous representation of the Lord we say we serve.

Even before we heard Trump's own confession of sexual criminality on the *Access Hollywood* tapes, he didn't seem too concerned about sexual assault, if a conviction might inconvenience him. In 1992, heavyweight boxing champion Mike Tyson was convicted of raping an eighteen-year-old woman. It happened to be inopportune timing for Trump. Tyson's next fight at Trump Plaza was slated to bring in millions. Trump had a personal interest in seeing Mike Tyson go free, so he held a press conference in an effort to strike a deal: if the prosecutors would let Mike Tyson go free, he would donate some of the proceeds from his fight to benefit victims of sex crimes. His ludicrous offer was widely condemned, and Mike Tyson was sentenced to prison.⁴

In the year prior to his election, Trump's campaign manager, Corey Lewandowski, grabbed a reporter by the arm and pulled her out of a press line. She had the bruises to show for it, but Lewandowski vehemently denied her claim. So did his boss. Without even bothering to ask her for her account, Trump heard Corey's denial and said the accusation could not be true because Lewandowski was a "very good person." He refused to consider it. But a camera on the property had captured the moment. The video footage showed the assault happened exactly as she had said. Charges were filed. Lewandowski, who was later charged with sexual assault in another case, finally apologized, but Trump never did.⁵

* * *

3. Claire Cohen, "Donald Trump Sexism Tracker: Every Offensive Comment in One Place," *Telegraph*, November 7, 2020, http://www.telegraph.co.uk/women/politics/donald-trump-sexism-tracker-every-offensive-comment-in-one-place.

4. Kranish and Fisher, *Trump Revealed*, 183.

5. Andrew Rafferty and Ali Vitali, "Trump Defends Campaign Manager Cory Lewandowski after Battery Charge," NBC, March 29, 2016, https://www.nbcnews.com/politics/2016-election/trump-campaign-manager-charged-assaulting-reporter-n547306.

Alexis Jones was a candidate on the television reality show *Survivor*. She is now a TV host and film producer, and the founder of I AM THAT GIRL, a nonprofit organization dedicated to the eradication of sexual assault and domestic violence. Alexis runs a program that reminds male athletes about what true manliness is, and how they have a mandate to protect women. Alexis travels to campuses all over the United States to visit locker rooms and share her message. Encouraged by men who have come forward to apologize to her, or have even started crying when she speaks, Alexis shares stories about real-life sisters and girlfriends and moms whose lives have been forever impacted by sexual assault. But occasionally her message is thwarted before she even has a chance to share it. Shortly after Trump took office, as she rounded the corner to speak to a room full of athletes, she was crushed to overhear the coach tell them, "We can grab women by the p***y now, because this is America."[6] For men like Trump, his election gave them permission.

It was while sitting in an evangelical church that I learned of the devil's timeless aggression toward women. It goes way back to the beginning.

> The LORD God said to the serpent,
> "Because you have done this,
> cursed are you above all the wild beasts
> and all the living creatures of the field!
> On your belly you will crawl
> and dust you will eat all the days of your life.
> And I will put hostility between you and the woman
> and between your offspring and her offspring;
> her offspring will attack your head,
> and you will attack her offspring's heel."[7]

Prostituted for a Platform

When a man belittles and mocks a woman, I get angry. Not just because I'm a woman, but because I have the spirit of the living Christ inside of me. So when Trump tweeted out, for the one hundredth time, yet another round of

---

6. Alexis Jones, "'Locker Room Talk.' Says Who?" YouTube, February 3, 2017, https://www.youtube.com/watch?v=lCA6EF3y23k.

7. Gen 3:14–15 NET.

disparaging, ugly words about a woman, it was like he was saying them to me. I saw red. I already knew how Jesus felt about the bullying, because I've read the Scriptures. So I waited for the male evangelical leaders to speak. Too many times I waited for an across-the-board, evangelical response that never came. Too many times I felt like one of Lot's daughters. Unworthy of defending. Prostituted for a political platform.

Physical and sexual abuse, and the bullying of women, doesn't seem to bother Donald Trump much, it doesn't seem to bother the coach in the locker room much, and in Trump's America, the world was left to wonder if it bothered Evangelicals much. Every pastor who has ever read the Bible should have recognized that the misogyny and abuse coming out of the White House was originating from an antichrist spirit (see Gen 3, above). When the church, who is supposed to be representing Jesus Christ, puts an abuser in the White House, and then goes dead silent and does not speak out when he actually abuses someone, the church is complicit. The Holy Spirit and the antichrist move in opposition to each other. By not opposing his words, pastor, you gave those words permission to keep going, grow, and cause harm (see Prov 18:21).

For me, the most damaging, depressing thing about the evangelical church falling in line behind Trump was not that we elected a bully. I can deal with that. Those men are everywhere, in leadership positions in government, corporations, educational and religious institutions, entertainment, sports, news, etc. Women are, unfortunately, used to navigating around creepy men. That doesn't hurt half as bad as learning that the men you did look up to—your fathers and brothers in the faith—are more like the coach in the locker room. Many of the men who should have done for us what Jesus did in the scene with the adulterous woman did not take the role of Jesus at all. They weren't the active stone throwers, but they didn't come to our defense, either. Too cowardly to step forward and stop it. Too "we must show respect to a man in a position of leadership" to confront the abuse. Just standing there, watching the rocks fly by.

Beth Moore echoed my thoughts on the deafening silence from the men:

> Wake up, Sleepers, to what women have dealt with all along in environments of gross entitlement & power. Are we sickened? Yes. Surprised? NO! Try to absorb how acceptable the disesteem and objectifying of women has been when some Christian leaders don't think it's that big a deal. . . . I'm one among many women

LEAVE HER ALONE

sexually abused, misused, stared down, heckled, talked naughty to. Like we liked it. We didn't. We're tired of it. . . .

"Keep your mouth shut or something worse will happen." Yes. I'm familiar with the concept. Sometimes it's terrifyingly true. Still, we speak.[8]

Julie Roys, evangelical journalist, podcaster, and radio talk show host who leads a ministry devoted to reporting the truth and restoring the church, had this to say: "I honestly don't know what makes me more sick. Listening to Trump brag about groping women or listening to my fellow evangelicals defend him."[9]

So here is the admonishment I offer to the male pastors and evangelical leaders who couldn't be bothered to rebuke our foul-mouthed president: I've spent twenty years in your churches, listening to you preach about how precious I am to God. A temple for the Holy Spirit. A new creation, radiant in Christ, transformed by the renewing of my mind. Special. Priceless. Worth a Son to him. And then all of a sudden someone attacks that priceless body, belittles that transformed mind, mocks that radiance—and that someone happens to be the president of the United States, the man you put on the throne of America for a political platform. And you go dead silent. Apparently my dignity isn't worth what I thought it was. My Jesus would have rebuked him. And if yours wouldn't, well, then I guess we are not following the same Christ. Mine can't be bought.

Meanwhile, the age-old war between Eve and the serpent wages on. And Eve's daughters are awake. You may even say they are infuriated. The continual bullying, the misogyny, the physical abuse, the sexual molestation, the fact that it's gone on largely uncontested by some leaders in the church—has awakened something powerful. A female army, empowered by the Holy Spirit, is rising up against the serpent, who has long made the abuse of women his favorite pastime. All this intercession on behalf of ourselves, and our sisters, has made our swords nice and sharp and polished. We are armed, we are ready, and we are dangerous to darkness. If there is one thing God's daughters learned the hard way with Trump's election, it's that if the snake is going to speak through a misogynistic bully in the White House, we are mostly going to have to defend ourselves.

---

8. Beth Moore (@BethMooreLPM), "Keep your mouth shut," Twitter, October 9, 2016, 8:32 a.m., https://twitter.com/BethMooreLPM/status/785141013085949952.

9. Julie Roys, "Evangelical Trump Defenders Are Destroying the Church's Witness," *Christian Post*, October 11, 2016, para. 2, https://www.christianpost.com/news/evangelical-trump-defenders-are-destroying-the-churchs-witness.html.

Gentlemen who rebuked Trump's abuse publicly, who effectively told him to "leave us alone," like my husband, my brother, pastors like Carlos Rodriguez and Jonathan Martin, Carlos Whittaker, Max Lucado, Eugene Cho, Napp Nazworth, Russell Moore, Bart Barber, and Rick Warren, we thank you. We see you, and we appreciate your Christlikeness. Evangelical leaders who didn't see this battle for what it was, don't bother getting up and dusting off your swords now. Woe to the shepherds who care more about protecting the bully than the bullied.

We'll take it from here.

The women . . . are a great army.[10]

---

10. Ps 68:11 NASB.

17

Lusting for Power

> You lust for what you don't have and are willing to kill to get it. You want what isn't yours and will risk violence to get your hands on it.—Jas 4:2

I come from a childhood home that was distrusting of religious people, and in many ways, that background has served me well. I believe that Christians should have to *earn* the world's trust. In our celebration over Donald Trump, we gave the world every good reason to distrust us. Heck, even *I* distrust the evangelical church now, and I'm a faith-filled, Bible-believing Jesus freak. The damage has been done. We burned our witness to the ground, and if we really want to rebuild, we should adopt a position of humility and ask God how to gain it back.

If God used Trump for anything, it was to show us what we look like to the rest of the world. God held up a mirror to the church, and Donald Trump looked back. God brought into the light what we needed to see about ourselves. I'm grateful. How else would I, would *we*, ever have known that some of us were essentially capable of indifference toward 800,000 Americans dead from a virus in twelve months? Or that some would be cool with separating young children from their parents? How else to learn that simply loving your neighbor and prioritizing their health would be considered "liberal" theology? Or that any in the church had it in them to unashamedly celebrate a man who called our fellow brethren "sons of bitches," "weak fools," and "human scum"? Or that some of our Christian friends would care more about Trump losing access to Twitter than him inciting a mob of violent people to commit a murderous and treasonous act? Now that we know what we are willing to partner with in order to gain control, what will we do with this information about ourselves? Will we be obstinate and arrogant in our ongoing quest for governmental power? Or will we do what the prophet Micah endorses: "To act justly and to love mercy and to walk humbly with your God?"[1]

"You Lust for What You Don't Have"

An unbridled lust for cultural, political, or religious dominance means we have fallen under the wrong spirit. It's a scheme of the enemy as old as the garden. He promises control, he promises power, he promises us a win in the "culture wars"—and then he convinces us that God wants us to have it. If the enemy can make us obsessed with having power, he will have achieved his goal of throwing us off mission.

God promises none of these things, because none of these things is necessary for our earthly assignment, which is simply to reconcile the world to a loving God by showing sacrificial love. God has a strategy for this reconciliation, and it has nothing to do with creating a "God-fearing nation" in which every constituent must comply with our beliefs. Rather, it has everything to do with creating an environment of love and compassion as we devote ourselves to welcoming the stranger, feeding the hungry, and standing alongside the oppressed. Giving God's kingdom away through acts of love and service is what blesses the heart of God.

In contrast, a quest for cultural dominance does not bless the heart of God. Worldly power has, over time, proven to be utterly detrimental to Christ followers, leading to attitudes of arrogance and superiority instead of Christlike humility and grace. Power has a corrupting influence, which can and *does* lead us away from our pure and simple devotion to Christ. In her profoundly timely and insightful book, *Celebrities for Jesus: How Personas, Platforms, and Profits Are Hurting the Church*, Katelyn Beaty observes that one of the great temptations of power is "to think that it can be used as a tool without it shaping and eventually disfiguring us in the process."[2]

---

1. Mic 6:8 NIV.

2. Katelyn Beaty, *Celebrities for Jesus: How Personas, Platforms, and Profits Are Hurting the Church* (Grand Rapids: Brazos, 2022), 165.

I quite think the Lord agrees. In fact, Christ cautioned his disciples about unchecked worldly power which would go to their heads:

> Jesus called them and said to them, "You know that those who are recognized as rulers of the Gentiles lord it over them, and those in high positions use their authority over them. *But it is not this way among you.* Instead whoever wants to be great among you must be your servant, and whoever wants to be first among you must be the slave of all. For even the Son of Man did not come to be served but to serve, and to give his life as a ransom for many."[3]

A pastor's kid who attended Bible college to become a missionary, writer D. L. Mayfield was born and raised evangelical. She never considered herself anything else, until she was forced to reevaluate what the term had become in light of support for Trump and Christian nationalism. She writes:

> I can no longer call myself an evangelical, because what defines a white evangelical in the United States has become a longing for an authoritarian state where Christianity is prioritized and privileged.
> This kind of Christian nationalism is entirely at odds with the gospel of Jesus, who told us right from the beginning that he was going to be good news to the poor, the imprisoned, the sick and the oppressed—and that he would be bad news for people who longed to clutch at power and safety and affluence at the expense of their neighbor.[4]

Like D. L. and millions of others who fled the evangelical church in the wake of Trumpism, Steve and I didn't leave Evangelicalism because we loved Jesus any less, or because we lost our commitment to his gospel. In fact, it was the exact opposite. We didn't like to see his message tarnished by what the term "evangelical" had come to mean.

Katelyn Beaty, who was raised in Evangelicalism and now says she has a "complicated" relationship with it, writes:

> The term "evangelical" has been sullied by political alliances, by a central whiteness and resistance to racial justice, by a leadership culture that seems to reward bullyish men and silences women.

---

3. Mark 10:42–45 NET; emphasis added.

4. D. L. Mayfield, "How a Sean Feucht Worship Service Convinced Me I Am No Longer an Evangelical," *Religion News Service*, September 23, 2020, para. 17, https://religionnews.com/2020/09/23/how-a-sean-feucht-worship-service-convinced-me-i-am-no-longer-an-evangelical/.

Debates ensue about whether racism and misogyny are features, or bugs of the movement....[5]

By now we've seen the wreckage left by the religious right's efforts: alliances with morally bankrupt politicians, a compromised public witness, and a generation of millennials who feel betrayed by their parents' generation and want nothing to do with their faith.[6]

I've wondered many times over the last several years, what would actually happen if the white evangelical church got everything it wanted in terms of political power and affluence and we got to, finally and irrevocably, enforce our beliefs on America. This seems to be the fantasy of many in the church, as if this is the end goal, even if, in exchange, we lose the trust of the world we are supposed to be winning. I envision what it would be like for us to be on top of a man-made hill, looking down on everyone else, thrusting our crosses, shooting our guns, and waving our American flags in tandem, high-fiving each other, hooting and hollering, "We finally did it! We owned the libs!"

Somehow, I don't think God would be proud. Christian domination over America may be the goal of many in the church, but it was never God's goal. When the world wants nothing to do with you, doesn't want to look like you, and, quite frankly, is in many ways more kind and gentle and compassionate than you are, what exactly is the draw for them? We can keep telling ourselves we are being persecuted for our beliefs. Or we can face the truth. Our salt is heavily contaminated by a pursuit of power. It tastes and smells rancid, because we have devoted ourselves to following conservative podcasters and commentators, instead of following Christ. In many cases, we have absorbed their attitudes of snarkiness and antagonism instead of Christ's attitude of gentleness and humility. We've meditated on their strategies for "owning the libs," instead of meditating on the Sermon on the Mount. The deafening cacophony of political noise has drowned out the soft whisper of the Holy Spirit.

Once salt loses its flavor, how can it be made salty again? Jesus's own strategy for achieving prominence and "greatness" looks a lot different than ours, and it also yields more actual results for the kingdom of God. In Jesus's kingdom, the way up is down. "Winning" looks a lot more like meekness, gentleness, and humility than "owning" one's political opponents. His is a

---

5. Beaty, *Celebrities for Jesus*, 24.
6. Beaty, *Celebrities for Jesus*, 155.

kingdom where we serve instead of dominate, we consider our neighbor as more important than ourselves (no matter their religious/sexual/political orientation), and we just love on people. That's how folks see Christ in us. When "winning" becomes more important than serving, somewhere along the way the children of God have lost the vision of God. I can guarantee that the people in my vision—waving their crosses and flags on a political hill that was gained only by rolling in the mud with Donald Trump—don't look like Christ to the rest of the world. It's one thing if political power comes to us decently and morally. But if we lust so much for what we don't have that we are willing to enable a man like Trump to get it, the world is right to question our judgment. About everything. Including the gospel.

This is what my parents saw early on in their church experience, which I didn't see until 2016. They saw an unquenchable desire for power and control. They saw pastors preach out of both sides of their mouth; one set of rules for the common folk and another set of rules for those in positions of influence. They saw Christians leave their integrity at the door as they went after power they assumed God wanted them to have. It's relatively easy to hide our lust for cultural dominance behind "pursuit of godly ideals."

Jesus didn't lust after political power because he didn't need it in order to do the job he was given. A more important and influential spiritual power came upon him as he grew in favor with God and man through his humble service to the poor, the broken, and the maligned.[7] It is written, however, that he had to pass a series of tests before he was endued with influential spiritual power from on high.[8] The last test came to him in the form of a political power grab.

> For the third test, the Devil took him to the peak of a huge mountain. He gestured expansively, pointing out all the earth's kingdoms, how glorious they all were. Then he said, "They're yours—lock, stock, and barrel. Just go down on your knees and worship me, and they're yours." Jesus's refusal was curt: "Beat it, Satan!"[9]

I believe God has called his children to change the world for the better. I believe God has power and influence for us, but it's a spiritual power, meant for service, and it will come only when we pass the test. If we want to give the world a true portrayal of Christ, the lust for political power is going to have to go. Also, we must take a lesson from Christ's

---

7. Luke 2:52; Phil 2:1–11.
8. Luke 4:1, 14.
9. Matt 4:8–10.

own example: never, ever, form a partnership with an unrepentant bully just to get what we want.

I challenge all of us to turn off the political commentators for a time and immerse ourselves in the love of God. Forsake ambition. Lay down our "rights." Simply embrace his lavish love, until we are drenched in it. When we are rested and refreshed by his voice and *only* his voice, we can go out and pour that immense love on our neighbors. And you know what, church?

We will change the world.

> Dear friends, let us love one another, because love is from God.[10]

---

10. 1 John 4:7.

18

Wisdom from Hell

> Such "wisdom" does not come down from heaven but is earthly, unspiritual, demonic. For where you have envy and selfish ambition, there you find disorder and every evil practice.—Jas 3:13–16

I've heard probably thousands of sermons in my twenty years' worth of active church attendance, but it wasn't until 2016, while praying through the distress in my spirit caused by the church's head-scratching infatuation with our chaos-causing president, that I became aware that there are two sources of wisdom. The more I studied, the more I couldn't believe that I've never heard a sermon, at least that I can recall, on the second source of "wisdom." It's a wisdom derived from hell, attained by people who have made a practice of listening to the wrong voice. Knowing that this is even possible really cleared up a lot of things for me. James writes:

> Who is wise and understanding among you? Let them show it by their good life, by deeds done in the humility that comes from wisdom. But if you harbor bitter envy and selfish ambition in your hearts, do not boast about it or deny the truth. Such "wisdom" does not come down from heaven but is earthly, unspiritual, demonic. For where you have envy and selfish ambition, there you find disorder and every evil practice.[1]

---

1. Jas 3:13–16 NIV.

Wow. Wow, wow, wow. I studied the verse in multiple translations to get a better idea of which characteristics may be observed in a person consistently listening to the wrong voice. A compilation of multiple translations lists them as: bitter speech, selfishness, vain conceit, boasting, denying truth, and constant disorder. These seemed to me to be the hallmarks of the Trump presidency. The verses caused me to think about how easy it would be for someone in a position of leadership, someone who exalted himself to that place by promising Evangelicals everything they ever wanted, to hide behind good-sounding promises while actually deriving wisdom from hell. Marked by selfish ambition and vain conceit, the negative effects of employing such a "wisdom" on America would be enormous and contagious. A person in a high position of authority who was getting their ideas from hell could cause untold confusion and chaos.

"Oh, What a Tangled Web We Weave / When First We Practise to Deceive"[2]

The premier way that hell's wisdom causes chaos is by the proliferation of lies. One of the most unfortunate consequences of Trump's presidency was the continual flood of lies and conspiracy theories that flowed like toxic waste from his mouth (or Twitter account), to the media outlets that pushed them, to, most unfortunate of all, many in the church who picked them up and passed them along. Politically, it started with Trump aggressively pushing the (racist) conspiracy theory that Barack Obama was born in Kenya. Five years later, he wouldn't let it go, and would not apologize when he was repeatedly proven wrong. The list of lies he either started or promoted since then is long and sordid, and some are so silly one can't imagine a grown adult thinking he could get away with such nonsense. From retweeting QAnon prophecies to PizzaGate to Ted Cruz's dad being involved in JFK's assassination, to American Muslims "celebrating" 9/11, to windmills causing cancer, fake terrorist attacks, fake migrant caravans, to the ridiculousness of Joe Scarborough murdering a staffer, or that Joe Biden organized the murder of members of SEAL Team Six and is controlled by people in "dark shadows," that the Ukrainian government is hiding a Democratic National Convention server, the unproven notion of hydroxychloroquine as a treatment for COVID-19, and the conspiracy

2. Sir Walter Scott, *Marmion: A Tale of Flodden Field* (Edinburgh: Archibald Constable, 1808), stanza 17.

theory that the 2020 election was rigged.³ It will take years to untangle the sticky messes made by Trump's webs of lies. He damaged people's lives as he spread foolish rumors about them, he riled up his followers with ridiculous nonsense that they in turn promoted as truth, and he undermined our democracy by convincing his most ardent supporters that our elections could not be trusted. Scripturally speaking, there is only one possible explanation for how a person could have such a high tolerance and capacity for lies. His ear is open 24/7 to their father.⁴

* * *

Renowned investigative journalist Bob Woodward has been a political reporter for fifty years, writing about nine presidents from Nixon to Trump.⁵ With the president's blessing and cooperation, he interviewed Donald Trump no less than seventeen times on the record for his book, *Rage*. Judging by the recordings transcribed in the book, the two men got along very well. Trump liked Woodward enough to grant him multiple interviews, and the conversations between them are cordial. Woodward is very fair, crediting Trump with exercising a somewhat successful, albeit highly unconventional, diplomacy with Kim Jong Un. He points out, however, that Trump has a hard time taking in information or relying on experts who tell him anything contrary to what he wants the truth to be. He makes up his own truth, which changes depending on his current mood, and expects the people around him to comply with his latest whim. For example, General James Mattis, Rex Tillerson, and Dan Coats, all conservatives, appeared to want nothing more than to help our country and assist our president in handling any crisis that arose. All of them are followers of God; in fact, Coats and Tillerson took the defense positions only because their wives told them God wanted them to. Each man is highly intelligent, devoted to our country, and strategic. But they were fired—impulsively, immaturely, and cruelly by tweet—because they refused to say just what Trump wanted to hear. They were fired for telling him the truth. The top national security leaders in our nation each came

---

3. Angelo Fichera and Saranac Hale Spencer, "Trump's Long History with Conspiracy Theories," FactCheck, October 20, 2020, https://www.factcheck.org/2020/10/trumps-long-history-with-conspiracy-theories/.

4. John 8:44 NIV.

5. Bob Woodward, *Rage* (New York: Simon & Schuster, 2020), 391.

away from their posts convinced that Donald Trump was not only unstable, but an incompetent, unfit, and dangerous threat to us.[6]

Another sign that someone is getting their wisdom from hell is the constant sowing of division and hate. Trump regularly appealed only to his base by insulting the rest of the country, thus giving his supporters permission to call them, among other names, "weak," "disgraceful," "human scum." Trump's spirit of disunity most assuredly doesn't come from spending time listening to God.

> Real wisdom, God's wisdom, begins with a holy life and is characterized by getting along with others. It is gentle and reasonable, overflowing with mercy and blessings, not hot one day and cold the next, not two-faced. You can develop a healthy, robust community that lives right with God and enjoy its results *only* if you do the hard work of getting along with each other, treating each other with dignity and honor.[7]

General James Mattis, Trump's secretary of defense who resigned in 2018 in protest over Trump's Syria policy, denounced him as a threat to our Constitution:

> Donald Trump is the first president in my lifetime who does not try to unite the American people—does not even pretend to try. Instead, he tries to divide us. We are witnessing the consequences of three years of this deliberate effort. We are witnessing the consequences of three years without mature leadership. We can unite without him, drawing on the strengths inherent in our civil society. This will not be easy, as the past few days have shown, but we owe it to our fellow citizens; to past generations that bled to defend our promise; and to our children.[8]

Besides lying and creating discord, another symptom of getting one's wisdom from hell is a selfish ambition that is the driving force behind every decision. It is noticeable to the reader of *Rage* that Trump has a hard time answering any of Woodward's questions on policy. He rambles and chatters incessantly, unfocused, until he can somehow bring the

---

6. Woodward, *Rage*, 387.

7. Jas 3:17–18; emphasis original.

8. Jeffrey Goldberg, "James Mattis Denounces President Trump, Describes Him as a Threat to the Constitution," *Atlantic*, June 3, 2020, para. 4, https://www.theatlantic.com/politics/archive/2020/06/james-mattis-denounces-trump-protests-militarization/612640/.

conversation back to the only thing he really seems to care about: himself, and his reelection. Bob Woodward writes of a conversation he had with Trump in February of 2020, in which the president bemoaned that in the course of his presidency, there was "dynamite behind every door." At the end of the book, Woodward reflects,

> But now, I've come to the conclusion that the "dynamite behind every door" was in plain sight. It was Trump himself. The oversized personality. The failure to organize. The lack of discipline. The lack of trust in others he had picked, the experts. The undermining or the attempted undermining of so many American institutions. The failure to be a calming, healing voice. The unwillingness to acknowledge error. The failure to do his homework. To extend the olive branch. To listen carefully to others. To craft a plan.[9]

Donald Trump is not just surrounded by chaos. Donald Trump *is* the chaos. For the duration of his presidency, that chaos radiated off of him in concentric circles, until it touched every single American life in an unhealthy way. On January 28, 2020, when he first got the news about the impact of the coming virus, Donald Trump did exactly what the Scripture says a person who gets their wisdom from hell would do. He selfishly considered himself first, and what it would mean for his presidency to be associated with an illness, which he thought would make him look "weak."[10] Next, he refused to listen to the experts who said he should take the virus seriously, that it had the potential to cost hundreds of thousands of lives, and that he should warn the American public. Donald Trump thought he could make the virus "disappear" by Easter simply by tweeting out the words. One minute he said masks were bad, and the next minute he said masks were good. Instead of telling the truth, which clearly is not his first language, Trump lied. In doing so, he fell flat in his duty to warn the American people of an oncoming crisis. And then to cover himself, he attempted to bully public health officials into supporting his messaging, and enlisted his most enthusiastic supporters to go along with the facade. Here, his contagion struck again. He was unsympathetic to the loss of life, so his followers were unsympathetic and found reasons to discount it. Despite downplaying the virus, Trump himself received the vaccine the moment it became available in January 2021, without telling his followers. He was happy to participate in something potentially

---

9. Woodward, *Rage*, 386.
10. Mary Trump, *Too Much*, 207.

lifesaving, while letting other people die for his cause. Hence the propaganda, lack of empathy, and COVID-19 deniers.

Wisdom from heaven is peace loving and pure. It tells the truth. It treats people with dignity and honor. It shows empathy. It brings people together in crisis. It does not seek to divide. It listens to people with more knowledge, because wisdom from heaven constantly seeks the greater good. But when a crisis comes to a person who is bloated with self-importance, who routinely provokes untruths and takes every opportunity to pit people against each other, then every conceivable type of disorder and evil will follow. In the midst of a public health crisis, Trump was not empowered from on high to bring peace, a sense of community, a sense of looking out for one's neighbors, and eventual healing. He was empowered from below to aggravate the situation by inserting even greater chaos, disunity, and heartlessness into it.

America knows very well what it looks like when a leader gets his "wisdom" from hell. It looks like 800,000 souls dead in nine months' time from an infection that could have been slowed by a reasonable, compassionate leader able to impart a gentle, merciful, kindhearted concern for one's neighbor.

19

Deborah's Daughters

> Villagers in Israel would not fight; they held back until I, Deborah, arose, until I arose, a mother in Israel.—Jdgs 5:7 NIV

I was serving on staff in a large nondenominational evangelical church with an all-male leadership team consisting of four pastors and ten elders. The entire ten years I worked there, it didn't occur to me to question their decision to leave women out of key leadership roles, because it appeared they had Scripture to back up their position. That is, I didn't question it until God started calling me to teach and preach.

Nearly every day when my children were small, I'd put them down for their naps and sneak into my closet with my Bible, a pen, and my prayer journal. I would pray, and then I recorded what I thought God was saying to me personally. If I felt he spoke to me through the Scriptures, I wrote it down. Over time, I started feeling like some of the verses he laid on my heart were not for me or my family, but for our church. Soon, I was filling up notebook after notebook of sermon material. One time, after sharing a few verses that I felt were specifically for our church with my direct supervising pastor, he suggested I deliver them to the congregation, not as a "sermon," but as a "word of encouragement."

I'll never forget what it felt like the night I stood before our church community to deliver the powerful word God had laid on my heart. I was allowed to do this only because it wasn't a normal Sunday service—it was a special worship night and the "rules" were more relaxed. I had listened intently to God, prayed about the message, went to my direct supervising pastor again for his confirmation and blessing, prepared and studied, all to deliver three or four sentences out of Habakkuk. That's how nervous I was and how special it was for me to be used by God in this manner.

I walked bravely to the stage, praying the entire time that God would use the Scriptures to impact our church body the way they had impacted me. I stepped up to the microphone, addressed my fellow congregants, took a deep breath, and started reading the paragraph I had prepared. As I began speaking, I sensed movement out of the corner of my eye. It was our senior teaching pastor. He was walking up the aisle toward the exit. He was a man who had several years of seminary under his belt, multiple theological degrees, and was someone I looked up to for scriptural knowledge. I had been in his office many times seeking biblical instruction. I considered him not just a pastor, but a friend. It struck me that I had sat under his sermons, taking notes, for hundreds of hours, and yet he couldn't give me the courtesy of five minutes. His doctrine had taught him that God wouldn't use a woman to speak publicly in church, therefore nothing I was about to say held value.

* * *

There is still, in many churches and religious institutions, a patriarchal mindset that seeks to push women back, and even silence them, and it doesn't come from God. Since the garden, the snake has worked overtime to shame, silence, and oppress women, while God has wanted to propel women forward—alongside men, not behind them. Women have special leadership skills necessary to advance the kingdom of God and to stomp out the enemy. In fact, some of the Bible's most celebrated women, including Deborah, Huldah, Jael, Junia, Lydia, Priscilla, and Phoebe, are leaders, evangelists, apostles, deacons, teachers of both women and men, heroines of war, and prophets. Consider God's servant Deborah. Deborah was a prophet, judge, military leader, and mother to Israel. She was chosen by God to lead, not because men were unavailable, but because she was the best person for the job.

As God's appointed commander-in-chief, Deborah had complete religious and civic authority to lead Israel's army into battle. Deborah received a message from God to deliver to Israel's military commander,

Barak. Deborah informed Barak that he was to lead the Israelite troops to the top of Mount Tabor, and at the same time, God would draw the enemy army to the river below and secure the win. Barak agreed to do it, but only if Deborah would accompany him. So Deborah said she would go, but that God would give the glory of the upcoming victory to a woman. That woman turned out to be Jael.

Deborah rode forth confidently into battle (giving Barak advice along the way). Meanwhile, Jael remained in her tent. To the enemy, she looked like any other nonthreatening, docile woman. But Jael was anything but docile. Behind the scenes, God had given her a wartime strategy for her dramatic role in history. God led the enemy's commander, Sisera, right to her, and she knew what to do. She invited him in, served him warm milk, and let him take a nap in her tent. Then, while he was asleep, she drove a tent peg through his skull.

By obeying God and taking their rightful positions in his kingdom, Jael and Deborah moved God's agenda forward, eliminated Israel's current enemy, and ushered in a reign of peace. The Bible records Deborah's victory song, in which Jael is called "most blessed."

> Most blessed of women be Jael,
> > the wife of Heber the Kenite,
> > most blessed of tent-dwelling women.
>
> He asked for water, and she gave him milk;
> > in a bowl fit for nobles she brought him curdled milk.
>
> Her hand reached for the tent peg,
> > her right hand for the workman's hammer.
>
> She struck Sisera, she crushed his head,
> > she shattered and pierced his temple. At her feet he sank,
> > he fell; there he lay.
>
> At her feet he sank, he fell;
> > where he sank, there he fell—dead.[1]

The spiritual implications are this: When women are allowed to take their proper positions, we will see more victories for the kingdom of God, more crushing of the serpent's head, and the church will move forward into her destiny. Likewise, when women are kept out of leadership and their voices go unheard, the church stalls. We are shutting the door of the

---

1. Jdgs 5:24–27.

kingdom of heaven in their faces by keeping them out of the portion of the kingdom that God has assigned to them. When only men are allowed to lead, it creates an imbalance of power that reinforces a patriarchal system of oppression. This systemic oppression is not only costing the church kingdom gains, it is costing the world.

While some Evangelicals have been working overtime to restrict and to silence women (partly by using New Testament Scripture out of context), Jesus has been propelling them forward. In fact, the first person he assigned to the task of evangelizing the good news of his resurrection was a woman.[2] Women, we must not settle for less than Christ died to give us. Rise up! Take your place. The world is waiting. Lead as you are called. Let Christ, not patriarchal religion, position you. God does not choose leaders based on gender. Like Deborah, Jael, Junia, Lydia, Priscilla, Esther, Mary, Abigail, and other celebrated women of the Bible, he chooses them based on anointing and faithfulness.

For every woman who has been shut down, demeaned, overlooked, or maligned by the religious patriarchy—rise up and take your place in God's kingdom. For every woman who has felt humiliated, defeated, and discouraged by the election of an abuser—rise up. Dust yourself off and do what God has called you to do. Do not neglect your gift. God rewards diligence and faithfulness. If you are an evangelist, evangelize. If you are a prophet, prophesy. If you are a teacher, teach. If you are called to preach and they won't let you preach at your church, do it anyway. Line up your kids' stuffed animals and practice preaching to them until God positions you in front of actual people. (Don't ask me how I know that!) Just *do* what you are called to do. This is how you drive the tent peg in. That is how you overcome the system of patriarchy that seeks to oppress. This is how you will help to clear a path for the generation of women leaders coming up behind us. And while you're at it, grab hands with a sister and encourage her in her unique gift. Women working together comprise a powerful army. Together, we can do what the men could not. Some battles are tailor made for the ladies. Just ask Deborah and Jael.

> "Of course I will go with you," Deborah answered, "but you will not get credit for the victory. The Lord will let a woman defeat Sisera."[3]

---

2. John 20:17.
3. Jdgs 4:9 NCV.

20

Lead Us Not

"They are loudmouths, full of hot air, but still they're dangerous. Men and women who have recently escaped from a deviant life are most susceptible to their brand of seduction. They promise these newcomers freedom, but they themselves are slaves of corruption, for if they're addicted to corruption—and they are—they're *enslaved*." —2 Pet 2:17–19

"WE HAVE JUST BEGUN TO FIGHT!!!"[1] Trump tweeted five weeks after the 2020 election, the day after the United States Supreme Court rejected his bid to overturn the election results. The Proud Boys and other far-right military extremist groups retweeted him with haste. For his niece, it came as no surprise that her uncle refused to accept his loss graciously and quietly; in fact, she had predicted the violence to come. "He's going to drag this out for as long as he's allowed to," she said. "He's stoking his followers into acts of violence. He's deliberately impeding the incoming administration."[2]

---

1. Donald J. Trump (@realDonaldTrump), "WE HAVE JUST BEGUN TO FIGHT!!!," Twitter, December 12, 2020, 5:47 a.m., https://twitter.com/realDonaldTrump/status/1337755964339081216.

2. "Donald Trump's Estranged Niece Says Uncle Is 'Deliberately' Refusing to Concede Election," CBC, November 15, 2020, para. 2, https://www.cbc.ca/news/politics/mary-trump-presidential-election-1.5802944.

Unfortunately, the warnings of Mary Trump and many others went unheeded by leaders in the Republican party, who, at that point, would have been the only ones with any power to step in and stop Trump's lies that the election had been "rigged." Instead, many of them insisted on going along with the ruse.[3] As a result, spurred on by false claims, and revved up by Trump's prior speech, a mob of his followers sieged the US Capitol building on January 6, 2021, intending to stop the certification of the election results. They were armed with guns, lead pipes, zip ties, explosives, tear gas, and a noose for Mike Pence (because he refused to go along with Trump's lie). Five people died, including a police officer, and multiple others were injured. It was an act of treasonous violence initiated by Trump's own lies, which were picked up and promoted by extremist propaganda, and carried out by people fully seduced, fully succumbed, and fully enslaved to Trump's violent agenda and his contagious spirit. Of the two thousand rioters, more than one thousand have been formally charged, and over five hundred have done prison time.[4] Even after sentencing, some held out hope for a Trump "pardon" that never came.[5]

Judge Timothy Kelly, appointed by Trump himself, concluded, "What happened that day was, in some ways, as serious . . . an offense as there can be, given that it threatened the peaceful transfer of power from one president to another. The damage that was done on that day was both tangible and intangible."[6] The judges in these cases have also agreed that being "sucked into a vortex of misinformation" does not excuse violent, criminal behavior.[7]

---

3. Martin Pengelly and Richard Luscombe, "'Complicit in Big Lie': Republican Senators Hawley and Cruz Face Calls to Resign," *Guardian*, January 10, 2021, https://www.theguardian.com/us-news/2021/jan/10/capitol-attack-republican-senators-josh-hawley-ted-cruz-face-resign.

4. Meg Anderson and Nick McMillan, "1,000 People Have Been Charged for the Capitol Riot. Here's Where Their Cases Stand," NPR, March 25, 2023, https://www.npr.org/2023/03/25/1165022885/1000-defendants-january-6-capitol-riot.

5. Gustaf Kilander, "QAnon Shaman Feels 'Duped' after Trump Doesn't Pardon Him: 'Only Thing Missing at Capitol Was Trump Stirring Up the Kool-Aid with a Big Spoon,' QAnon Shaman's Lawyer Says," *Independent*, January 22, 2021, https://www.independent.co.uk/news/world/americas/qanon-jacob-chansley-arrest-trump-pardon-b1791365.html.

6. Anderson and McMillan, "1,000 People," para. 16.

7. Anderson and McMillan, "1,000 People," para. 17.

James says, "God is impervious to evil, and puts evil in no one's way. The temptation to give in to evil comes from us and only us. We have no one to blame but the leering, seducing flare-up of our own lust."[8]

The riot was condemned by leaders worldwide as a disgraceful attack that conjured up the words of British philosopher John Stuart Mill: "Bad men need nothing more to compass their ends, than that good men should look on and do nothing."[9] But for those paying attention to the warnings all along, the violence and chaos of the insurrection was highly predictable. Good men and women did try to stop it, but the groundwork had been laid long ago. It was the inevitable outcome of too many people willing to get behind a man whose lust for power has dominated him his entire life.

A Slave to Corruption

To understand the end, it's important to go back to the beginning. Donald's childhood and his relationship with his father, Fred, explains a lot. Mary Trump explains her grandfather Fred was a sociopath who cared only about his own self-interest, and nothing about his family, except for what achievements they could lend to the family name. Fred Trump controlled and manipulated his wife and his children (and grandchildren) using threats over money. If they didn't do exactly what he wanted them to do, he berated them and cut them off completely. For example, he would pay for their education, but it had to be the school of his choice. Fred Trump enjoyed holding power over people, and sadistically, he liked watching them beg for things. Mary attributes this as the reason her dad (Donald's older brother Freddy) died of complications from alcoholism at forty-three. No matter what Freddy did, he could never please his dad. Fred also refused to acknowledge sickness, weakness, or emotion, and was indifferent to the needs of others. The only values he possessed were toward business and wealth, and it didn't matter to him how many people were hurt, or how many workers went unpaid, or how many laws were broken, in order for that wealth to accumulate. He sued anyone who got in his way and held in contempt any truth that didn't flatter him.

With a harsh, unloving father, and a mom sick in bed due to chronic illnesses, Donald suffered through childhood desperate for attention. But the

---

8. Jas 1:13–15.

9. John Stuart Mill, Oxford Reference, February 1, 1867, quote 6, https://www.oxfordreference.com/display/10.1093/acref/9780191843730.001.0001/q-oro-ed5-00007298.

only time he got it was when he bullied his brothers or called women names at the dinner table. According to Mary, those were the types of behaviors that caught his dad's attention and earned Donald the recognition he so desperately craved. He was berated if he showed any signs of weakness, so he learned, partially by watching how his dad treated Freddy, not to. Mary Trump says Donald's pitiable relationship with his father left him stunted, "incapable of growing, learning, or evolving, unable to regulate his emotions, moderate his responses, or take in and synthesize information."[10]

When Donald took over the family business, Mary observed that his belligerence and his penchant for blaming other people surpassed even her grandfather's. He mismanaged corporations, ran several casinos into the ground, and declared one bankruptcy after another, but Fred swooped in time and again to save him and rescue the family name. Donald learned to sue in order to get what he wanted, and if someone sued him, he just counter-sued. So Donald's refusal to admit defeat in business was not only tolerated, but fostered. Loss was simply not an option for someone trained to be a "winner" at any cost. Mary writes, "Fred came to appreciate Donald's obstinacy because it signaled the kind of toughness he sought in his sons. . . . This is the end result of Donald's having continually been given a pass and rewarded not just for his transgressions—against tradition, against decency, against the law, and against fellow human beings. The lies may become true in his mind as soon as he utters them, but they're still lies. It's just another way for him to see what he can get away with."[11]

This explains why, when his desperate efforts to overturn the election failed and Joe Biden's win was officially confirmed, Donald set about making the transition as indecorous as he possibly could manage. He promoted QAnon election conspiracy theories, which were picked up by his followers, he called people who trusted the results "weak fools," and he appeared at several "rallies" . . . to keep his most stalwart fans inspired so that they wouldn't have to face the truth of his defeat, and also so they would continue to send him money. In early January 2021, just days prior to the insurrection, Trump attempted to blackmail Georgia's secretary of state into "finding" more votes for him.[12] When that didn't work, he egged on

10. Mary Trump, *Too Much*, back cover.
11. Mary Trump, *Too Much*, 204–5.
12. Amy Gardner, 'I Just Want to Find 11,780 Votes': In Extraordinary Hour-Long Call, Trump Pressures Georgia Secretary of State to Recalculate the Vote in His Favor," *Washington Post*, January 3, 2021, www.washingtonpost.com/politics/trump-raffensperger-call-georgia-vote/2021/01/03/d45acb92-4dc4-11eb-bda4-615aaefd0555_story.html.

his most enthusiastic supporters toward violence, because he would rather see chaos and bloodshed in these United States than admit his defeat. And chaos and bloodshed is what he got.

Donald loves to wreak havoc. Havoc is what has gotten him attention his entire life, first from Fred at the family dinner table, then in business, and then from the world. Like his father before him, he also derives pleasure from making people squirm under his lordship. He would much prefer to go golfing and let peoples' unemployment benefits expire (another lesson learned from Fred: make them beg for it!) than sign a bill to bring relief to millions of suffering people.[13]

Boasting about himself incessantly and causing turmoil for others is how Donald Trump was raised. He has made a life and a name for himself based on those two attributes, and those two attributes alone also entirely dismiss him from the Lord's service. They counter any notion that he is, or ever was, anointed by God. In fact, the Bible says of such men, "These people are grumblers and fault-finders who go wherever their desires lead them, and they give bombastic speeches, enchanting folks for their own gain . . . propelled by their own ungodly desires. These people are divisive, worldly, devoid of the Spirit."[14]

"Be as Wise as a Serpent and as Innocent as a Dove"[15]

If the evangelical church thinks that the world can be easily deceived, but we in the church cannot—there has been a grave misunderstanding of Scripture. There are multiple New Testament warnings against falling for the schemes of con men, and they are directed toward people of God.

Danger doesn't always come from where we expect it to. The enemy is going to wave his arms around and jump around like crazy to try to get us to focus on some perceived danger from "outsiders," "dems," "libs," "socialists," "communists," or whatever the bogeyman of the day is. But actual danger—true, spiritual danger—doesn't do a song and dance routine right in front of you. Real danger hides, it lurks, it prowls, and it infiltrates. It very often comes from within our own tribe, or perhaps a recent convert to our tribe.

---

13. Tami Luhby et al., "Unemployment Benefits Lapse for Jobless Americans as Trump Holds Out on Signing Relief Bill," CNN, December 27, 2020, https://www.cnn.com/2020/12/26/politics/unemployment-benefits-stimulus-relief-bill/index.html.

14. Jude 16, 18–19 NET.

15. Paraphrase of Matt 10:16.

Danger poses as someone we trust, someone who is on our side, someone who says he's there to "help" or "rescue" us. Church, I say this with all gentleness and respect: the real danger is not coming from the world. Very often, it's in your own conservative church community. Look at what is happening in the SBC right now. Another case in point: while white Evangelicals spent the last two decades tearing their hair out over the threat of Islamic terrorism, they were growing "Christian" nationalist terrorists in their own backyards. See video from January 6, 2021, for evidence.

Sometimes you have to think like a snake.[16] If I was a snake, I would want to lead the twenty-first century church *away* from the powerful gospel of Jesus Christ. I'd employ the spirit of Judas to contaminate their witness so that they would lose their integrity, their dignity, and ultimately, their harvest. That would be well achieved by tempting them into an alliance with a false leader, someone who the rest of the world could easily and rightly peg as a slave to corruption. I'd tempt them into this unholy alliance by dangling a carrot. There is one no-fail, surefire thing that would make them bite: a conservative, pro-life political platform.

There are approximately one hundred verses that warn the church away from dangerous false leaders. If the church wants the world to take *us* seriously, then we need to take those verses seriously. Do a Bible Gateway search of "false leader," and read through the descriptive warnings. There is no one on earth who fulfills those warnings more perfectly than Donald Trump. If we read them soberly, with humility, and with a desire for truth as our ultimate goal, we may even conclude that posing an easy target like Donald Trump as "God's chosen" was a plan of the serpent all along. Trump's childhood made him vulnerable, his arrogance made him willing, and his lack of repentance made him cooperative. "For such people are false apostles, deceitful workers, disguising themselves as apostles of Christ. And no wonder, for even Satan disguises himself as an angel of light. Therefore it is not surprising his servants also disguise themselves as servants of righteousness, whose end will correspond to their actions."[17] All the warning signs were there. He came for the church, he promised us the world, and then he cast his spell. We lusted for the power we didn't have and took him up on the offer.

Let us pray.

---

16. Matt 10:16.

17. 2 Cor 11:12–15.

LEAD US NOT

Our Father in heaven,
hallowed be your name,
your kingdom come,
your will be done,
on earth as it is in heaven.
Give us today our daily bread.
And forgive us our debts,
as we also have forgiven our debtors.
And lead us not into temptation,
but deliver us from the evil one.[18]

---

18. Matt 6:9–13 NIV.

21

Be Zealous and Repent

> Those whom I love, I reprove and discipline; therefore be zealous and repent.—Rev 3:19 NASB

It's not wrong to want unborn babies to have a chance at life. It's not wrong to want a strong military and protected borders. It's not wrong to want a healthy economy and high-paying jobs. It is wrong if we have to align ourselves with evil in order to get those things. It is wrong if we have to excuse abuse, misogyny, sexism, racism, violence, perversion, and lies. It is wrong, if, in pursuit of the good, we preach morality at the same time we align ourselves with the blatantly immoral. The Bible has a word for the giving up of one's dignity, respect, and integrity in exchange for a commodity (or platform). It's called prostitution. "Therefore repent and turn back so that your sins may be wiped out, so that times of refreshing may come from the presence of the Lord, and so that he may send the Messiah appointed for you—that is, Jesus."[1]

Repentance—what a wonderful concept. It literally means "to change one's mind." And the promise attached to repentance is even more extraordinary—a "time of refreshing" will come. Some call that time of refreshing "revival."

I've been fascinated with the idea of revival for about ten years now—ever since God physically healed me. The whole idea that he could burst

---

1. Acts 3:19–20 NET.

into our lives at any moment—that he could show up in our lives with his goodness and life and all kinds of healing power—it floors me. I believe God wants to "break through" more often than we let him, and that what holds him back is not his lack of desire to save, heal, and deliver, but the church's own lust for power and control.

I've had a small, personal taste of the spiritual refreshing Acts 3:19 refers to. A few years ago, two girlfriends and I took a road trip south to visit a church known for its revival mentality and powerful moves of the Holy Spirit. I was nervous, but excited. We had heard that the church held a Saturday prayer session in advance of the service on Sunday, so we went to check it out. It was very informal. Probably fifty people or so were there, sitting, standing, and praying in a large room while the worship band played. (I couldn't believe they had a worship band there just for Saturday prayer!) It was a soft, inviting atmosphere and my girlfriends and I just stood with our hands up and soaked in the music. Suddenly, mid-song, the trumpet player stopped playing. I opened my eyes and looked up. He walked off the stage, right toward us. For some reason, he was staring right at me. I looked around, wondering if there was a person standing near me that he was aiming for, but he strolled up, like a man on a mission, and said in broken English that God had told him to play his trumpet over me. I was so bewildered I just stood there. I couldn't move or speak. He prayed a beautiful prayer (it sounded beautiful, anyway—it was in Norwegian), that I couldn't understand with my ears but somehow felt in my spirit. The band on stage had stopped playing and turned their attention to where I was standing with the trumpet player. The whole room was watching. I'm sure my face was red, but I didn't have time to be embarrassed because everything happened so fast and because I was so touched. Then he played his trumpet right next to me. It sounded like a kind of commissioning. And you will never guess what happened next.

I turned into a four-year-old. I took off running around the perimeter of the room. I was crying and laughing at the same time, but mostly laughing. I may have spun a few circles. (This is way out of character for me, I am normally quite reserved, especially in front of people. I never do outlandish things!) My girlfriends were still at the front by the stage, watching and cracking up. When I got back to them, I grabbed them and made them run with me. It was so fun! And the best part is that people were laughing along with us. No one seemed to think it was all that weird. It felt like heaven had dropped into the room. Jesus was there and we were overflowing with joy! We ran around and giggled until we literally ran out of steam, and all the while, the trumpet played on. The whole scene was 2 Cor 3:17 in action. "Now the Lord is the Spirit, and where the Spirit of the Lord is, there is freedom."

I think I learned more about Jesus—and his radical energy, passion, and joy—in that twenty-minute personal revival than in twenty years of traditional church teaching. Don't get me wrong, I love Bible study and teaching. It's just that sometimes we forget that it is his actual presence and power that transforms us. And it is his presence working through us that will change the world. Christians have a mandate to bring heaven to earth. When it comes to real, lasting change in America, the truth is that forcing a conservative mindset and Republican legislation will never bring it. But Jesus will.

God did not decree the Trump presidency; he allowed it. That's how much he loves his church. Because now we can take a good, long, hard, honest look at ourselves. We can look at the man we elected, and celebrated, and see how far away we are from looking like Jesus. We can stop asking ourselves why it's so hard to get people to come to church with us.

The spirit of betrayal that tempted Judas can tempt anyone. It values rules and regulations and conformity over loving people. In some churches, it validates white supremacy and oppresses women. It is greedy. It's narcissistic, controlling, authoritarian, and judgmental. It manipulates. In varying degrees throughout the church, it is perverse, dehumanizing, abusive, sexist, and arrogant. It covers up evil, usually using Scripture applied wrongly. It acts superior. It seeks praise and glory for itself. It needs to be repented of, by all of us.

If we respond rightly to God, the church's greatest days are ahead of her. A broken church, a humble church, a church on her knees, casting down every idol of control and fear and quest for worldly dominance, could be a glorious thing. There is only one thing we can do. "If my people, who are called by my name, will humble themselves and pray and seek my face and turn from their wicked ways, then I will hear from heaven, and I will forgive their sin and will heal their land."[2]

I want healing in our land. I've had a brief, personal taste of God's presence and freedom, and ten years later, it's all I can think about. I want more. And so, I regularly repent. Please join me if you will.

---

2. 2 Chron 7:14 NIV.

> Lord, thank you for your rescue. Forgive me for my own snarkiness and bad attitude toward those who don't share my same beliefs. Allow me to go forward with kindness, with an ear bent toward compassion and understanding, and to value diversity of thought and opinion over getting my own way. I repent of an unholy alliance made with a dangerous and contagious leader. I ask for your cleansing truth to reveal the damage done to our witness, and your extravagant grace to repair it. May our hearts come into alignment with yours, and may your church be built up into maturity in Christ, with a diligence toward recognition of false prophets who may tempt us in the future. Let us be tempted by Christ's love and Christ's power alone. In Jesus's name. Amen.

With the casting down of idols and the return to God's actual presence and power, we really can be a light to the world. We are never going to agree on every issue, but we can agree, in our relationships with one another, to "have the same mindset as Christ Jesus,"[3] which is to choose humility, tenderness, and compassion. As his disciples, we will never go wrong if we do this. Across these United States, let us drop our insults and our quarrelsomeness, and let us eschew affiliation as "red" or "blue," as we seek to simply be affiliated with Christ. Let us be peacemakers whose aim is not to "rule the land" but to sow peace. In this way we will resemble the Lord we serve and make his joy complete.

> Therefore if you have any encouragement from being united with Christ, if any comfort from his love, if any common sharing in the Spirit, if any tenderness and compassion, then make my joy complete by being like-minded, having the same love, being one in spirit and of one mind. Do nothing out of selfish ambition or vain conceit. Rather, in humility value others above yourselves, not looking to your own interests but each of you to the interests of the others.[4]

From sea to shining sea, a wave of nationwide repentance sweeping across the evangelical church in America could actually lead to a real revival marked by humility. May we embrace each other's differences in love, and experience a peaceful spirit of unity as we come together, in true brotherhood and sisterhood, under the beauty of God's grace.

---

3. Phil 2:5 NIV.
4. Phil 2:1–4 NIV.

O beautiful for spacious skies,
For amber waves of grain,
For purple mountain majesties
Above the fruited plain!
America! America!
God shed his grace on thee
And crown thy good with brotherhood
From sea to shining sea![5]

---

5. Katharine Lee Bates, "America the Beautiful." For background, see "America the Beautiful," Library of Congress, 2002, https://www.loc.gov/item/ihas.200000001/.

Epilogue

What an emotional roller coaster these last seven years have been. I started writing this book in 2016, as a way to process my thoughts with God about the evangelical church's triumphant celebration of a man I considered to be spiritually dangerous. I didn't know if it would ever see the light of day, and I wasn't always sure I wanted it to. I asked God not to release it unless and until 1) it would honor him, and 2) I was strong enough spiritually and emotionally to handle the inevitable backlash. My aim was to tell the truth by being vulnerable and forthright.

Twenty-three years ago, with a glad and trusting heart, I let the white American evangelical church take me by the hand and lead me around. We covered a lot of sacred ground. She led me to the gospel of Jesus Christ, which has been the greatest gift I've ever received, and is the guiding force of truth through which everything else in my life must be measured. I could not possibly be more grateful for this gift. We traveled to other places together too. Through the books I read and courses I undertook under the counsel of the church, I became a pretty good model of evangelical ideology. I trekked with the church through *The Purpose Driven Life*. I hiked around from Christian marriage conferences to Christian parenting conferences and traveled the rocky road of *Love and Respect*.[1] I followed the prescribed method for how to love a husband who was *Wild at Heart*.[2]

---

1. Emerson Eggerichs, *Love and Respect* (Nashville: Thomas Nelson, 2005).

2. John Eldredge, *Wild at Heart: Discovering the Secret of a Man's Soul* (Nashville: Thomas Nelson, 2022).

EPILOGUE

I learned how to be *The Excellent Wife*.[3] (Although that one damn near killed me.) Steve Hawk courageously scaled the rough terrain of the *Love Dare*—twice.[4] I was *Breaking Free* while I was *Believing God*.[5] I survived a lot of VBS. I set my young kids down in front of the TV to watch *Bibleman* and *Veggie Tales*.[6] I budgeted to the last dime to send them to private Christian schools. Through the hills and valleys of the evangelical landscape, I was mentored, cared for, discipled, loved. When I was diagnosed with skin cancer at thirty-nine and had to have surgery, I was prayed over, anointed with oil, and fed multitudes of delicious casseroles in my recovery. This pilgrim is grateful for her journey.

I let the evangelical church lead me until she took me to a place I couldn't follow. My heart was devastated in the letting go. I had to say goodbye to a church community I loved, a pastor I adored, and another pastor I thought of as a spiritual father. It was an agonizing and disorienting time. I lost friends; some I had been friends with for over twenty years. I didn't fault them. I'd run with the evangelical pack for so long, and now I was going against the grain. Every element of instruction I received while under evangelical tutelage was put under a microscope and inspected. My faith itself underwent a great shaking, and many of my long-held beliefs fell away. You know what though?

Jesus held.

---

3. Martha Peace, *The Excellent Wife: A Biblical Perspective* (Bemidji, MN: Focus, 1999), rev. ed.

4. Stephen Kendrick and Alex Kendrick, *The Love Dare* (Nashville: B&H, 2013), rev. ed.

5. Beth Moore, *Breaking Free: Discover the Victory of Total Surrender* (Nashville: B&H, 2007), rev. ed.; Beth Moore, *Believing God Day by Day: Growing Your Faith All Year Long* (Nashville: B&H, 2008).

6. Tony Salerno, creator, *Bibleman*, aired 1995–2010, on Australian Christian Channel; Phil Vischer and Mike Nawrocki, creators, *Veggie Tales*, first released December 21, 1993, by Big Idea.

Recommended Reading

Anyabwile, Thabiti. "4 Problems Associated with White Evangelical Support of Donald Trump." *Gospel Coalition*, November 9, 2016. https://www.thegospelcoalition.org/blogs/thabiti-anyabwile/4-problems-associated-with-white-evangelical-support-of-donald-trump/.
Blow, Charles M. "White Evangelicals Shun Morality for Power." *New York Times*, September 19, 2021. https://www.nytimes.com/2021/09/19/opinion/white-evangelical-politics.html.
Cheney, Liz. *Oath and Honor: A Memoir and a Warning*. New York: Little, Brown, 2023.
Cho, Eugene. *Thou Shalt Not Be a Jerk: A Christian's Guide to Engaging in Politics*. Colorado Springs: Cook, 2020.
French, David. "Evangelicals Are Supporting Trump Out of Fear, Not Faith." *Time*, June 27, 2019. https://time.com/5615617/why-evangelicals-support-trump/.
Galli, Mark. "Trump Should Be Removed from Office." *Christianity Today*, December 19, 2019.
Harper, Lisa Sharon. *The Very Good Gospel: How Everything Wrong Can Be Made Right*. Colorado Springs: Penguin Random House, 2016.
Hassen, Steve. *The Cult of Trump: A Leading Cult Expert Explains How the President Uses Mind Control*. New York: Simon & Schuster, 2019.
Kranish, Michael, and Marc Fisher. *Trump Revealed: An American Journey of Ambition, Ego, Money, and Power*. New York: Scribner, 2016.
Kobes de Mez, Kristin. *Jesus and John Wayne: How White Evangelicals Corrupted a Faith and Fractured a Nation*. New York: Liveright, 2020.
Lucado, Max. "Trump Doesn't Pass the Decency Test." *Washington Post*, February 26, 2016. https://www.washingtonpost.com/posteverything/wp/2016/02/26/max-lucado-trump-doesnt-pass-the-decency-test/.
Nazworth, Napp. "Evangelicals Trade Moral Authority for Political Gain in Defending Trump." *Christian Post*, February 6, 2019. https://www.christianpost.com/news/evangelicals-trade-moral-authority-for-political-gain-in-defending-trump.html.

RECOMMENDED READING

Ross Range, Peter. "The Theory of Political Leadership that Donald Trump Shares with Adolf Hitler." *Washington Post*, July 25, 2016. https://www.washingtonpost.com/posteverything/wp/2016/07/25/the-theory-of-political-leadership-that-donald-trump-shares-with-adolf-hitler/.

Sider, Ronald J., ed. *The Spiritual Danger of Donald Trump: 30 Evangelical Christians on Justice, Truth, and Moral Integrity*. Eugene, OR: Cascade, 2020.

Snyder, Timothy. *On Tyranny: Twenty Lessons for the Twentieth Century*. New York: Crown, 2017.

Sullivan, Amy. "America's New Religion: Fox Evangelicalism." *New York Times*, December 15, 2017. https://www.nytimes.com/2017/12/15/opinion/sunday/war-christmas-evangelicals.html.

Trump, Mary L. *Too Much and Never Enough: How My Family Created the World's Most Dangerous Man*. New York: Simon & Schuster, 2020.

Wallis, Jim. *Christ in Crisis: Why We Need to Reclaim Jesus*. San Francisco: HarperCollins, 2019.

Wehner, Peter. "Why I Can No Longer Call Myself an Evangelical Republican." *New York Times*, December 9, 2017. https://www.nytimes.com/2017/12/09/opinion/sunday/wehner-evangelical-republicans.html.

Acknowledgments

To my family, Steve, Savanna, and Cruise: your continual love and support mean the world to me. I'm sorry about all the bad dinners. I love you all so much!

Steve, there is no one else on earth with whom I would rather be on this grand adventure than with you. You encouraged me to write this book from the get-go, even though it would have been so much easier to set it aside. Your steadfast determination is contagious, and I'm so lucky to call you mine!

To Shelley Morgan, my long-distance prayer partner, Bible study bestie, shopping buddy and all-around sounding board. God knew what he was doing when he brought us together again after twenty-plus years of friendship! I'm so thankful for your strength, your wisdom, and your constant encouragement. Thank you for studying Galatians with me, and for insisting that I *keep going*! I love you!

To Susan Wade: You are an incredible high school English and AP history teacher, and I am your willing student! Your editing, wisdom, and feedback as a pastor's wife who has spent a lot of time in evangelical spaces was invaluable to me. I am so blessed by your friendship and grateful for your devotion to this project.

To my cheerleaders and prayer partners who believed in this book from its inception, and encouraged me to persevere when I might have otherwise given up: Dana Richardson, Deanna Bax, Sheila Kay, Jen Bergman, Lisa Saunders, and Carol Helland; I have no doubt that your intercession made this book possible. You are each strong women of valor. I'm so thankful for and inspired by your strength.

Dr. James Brauer: It was not a coincidence when God sent me to work in your office. Not only did I get a great job, I got a great boss who would become my encourager, my sometime pastor, and my friend. Your support and your willingness to assist with editing have been an invaluable blessing to me. I'm forever thankful.

Last, I prayed that God would provide a wise and thoughtful editor, one who could challenge as well as inspire me. Thank you, Charlie Collier! You and Matthew, and Shannon and Zechariah, and the entire team at Cascade Books, were an answer to my prayers. What an incredible experience and amazing team!

Subject Index

Access Hollywood, 44, 75, 108
Acosta, Jim, 33, 33n19
Alcindor, Yamiche, 26
Antipas, Herod, 35–39, 81–83, 85–86
Apprentice, 47, 67
Arpaio, Joe (Sheriff), 67, 67n78
Art of the Deal, 54n16, 61, 61n46

Barber, Bart, 112
Barr, Bill, 60
Barrett, Wayne, 63
"Barron, John," 58, 72
Bassett, John, 63
Beaty, Katelyn, 114–16, 114n2
Bethel Church, 4
Biden, Joe, 93n9, 120, 132
Bishop Curry, Michael, 101
Blackwell, Victor, 65
Brzezinski, Mika, 23, 26, 62n49, 107
"Bully-ruler," xvi–xviii

Carlson, Tucker, 10
Carroll, E. Jean, xii, 46, 46n17, 47, 47n18
Case For Christ, 3, 3n1
Celebrities for Jesus, 114, 114n2, 116n5, 116n6
Central Park Five,
    McCray, Antron, 66

Richardson, Kevin, 66
Salaam, Yusef, 66
Santana, Raymond, 66
Wise, Korey, 66
Chao, Elaine, 22, 22n6, 26, 95
Charlottesville, West Virginia, 38, 54, 67–68
Christian Nationalism, 115
Christie, Chris, 56
Cho, Eugene, 112
Claiborne, Shane, 103, 103n1
Clinton, Bill, 42
Clinton, Hillary, 94
Coats, Dan, 60, 121
Cohen, Michael, 24, 60
Collins, Gail, 107
COVID, 40–41, 84, 120, 124
Cruz, Carmen Yulin, 26, 107
Cruz, Heidi, 56
Cruz, Ted, 56, 120, 130n3
Curiel, Judge Gonzalo, 67
Cult, 9, 16–19, 17n16–17, 18n20, 31

D'Antonio, Michael, 58n29, 64–65, 64n62, 68n83
Deborah, 125–28
Duke, David, 97

SUBJECT INDEX

Educated, 18, 18n19
Esther, 128
Esther, Elizabeth, 17–18, 18n18
Evangelism Explosion, 3–4

False Leader (Prophet, Teacher), 18, 49, 72–74, 134
False Messiah, ix, 12–19, 64
Falwell, Jerry Jr., 14, 31
Fahrenthold, David, 34
Feucht, Sean, 115n4
Financial Peace University, 5
Fiorina, Carly, 107
"Fox Evangelicalism," 59n35
Fox News, 24–25, 42, 84, 84n7
Focus on the Family, 42

Girl at the End of the World, 18, 18n18
Goff, Bob, 20, 20n1
Gothard, Bill, 31
Graham, Franklin, 5, 14

Hanoi Hilton, 5, 27, 80, 95
Harris, Kamala, 26
Hillsong Church, 31
Hilton, Paris, 44–45, 45n11
Hitler, Adolf, 50–74
Hitler, Alois, 58
Hubbard, L. Ron, 17, 19, 73
Huffington, Arianna, 107
Hutchinson, Christopher, 84, 84n6

Iscariot, Judas, Author's note, xi–xiii, 25, 45, 97, 106, 134, 138

Jeffress, Pastor Robert, 14, 14n8
Jekyll and Hyde, 57
John the Baptist, 35, 38, 101
Jones, Alexis, 109, 109n6
Jones, Jim, 19, 73

Kelly, Megyn, 23–26, 23n7, 32, 34, 107
King Cyrus, xv
King Jeroboam, 82
King, Martin Luther Jr., Dr., 72
King Nebuchadnezzar, 25, 97
King Saul, 25

KKK, 54, 54n19, 67, 67n75
KKK for Trump, 67
Koresh, David, 19

Lalich, Janja, 18, 18n20
Letters From a Skeptic, 5, 5n3
Lewandowski, Corey, 108, 108n5
Liberty University, 31
Lohan, Lindsay, 46, 46n12
Lucado, Max, 112

Machado, Alicia, 56, 107
Mandela, Nelson, 72
Maples, Marla, 56
Mars Hill Church, 31
Martin, Jonathan, 112
Mattis, General James, 22, 60, 94, 121–22, 122n8
Mayfield, D. L., 115, 115n4
McConnell, Mitch, 22, 22n6, 94–95, 94n15
Mein Kampf, 62
Mill, John Stuart, 131, 131n9
Miscavige, David, 17, 19, 73
Misogyny, misogynistic, xii, xiii, 26, 45, 47, 70, 76, 92, 97, 110–11, 116, 136
Moore, Beth, 5, 45, 45n8, 110, 111n8, 142n5
Moore, Russell, Dr., 112
Morning Joe, 62n49, 32
Mulvaney, Mick, 60

Nassar, Larry, 31
Nationalism, nationalist, 30, 89, 89n5, 115, 134
Nazi, Nazism, 14n8, 19, 38, 42, 51, 53–54, 67, 95
Nazworth, Napp, 112
Nixon, Richard, 121
NXIVM, 17, 17n16

Obama, Barack, 8, 70, 70n91, 92, 120
Obama, Michelle, 61
O'Donnell, Rosie, 107
Oxenberg, Catherine, 17, 17n17

SUBJECT INDEX

Pence, Mike, 60, 93, 96, 130
Peterson, Eugene, 30
Pizzagate, 120
Playboy, 42, 47, 68, 68n85
Polygamist's Daughter, 18, 18n19
Posner, Sarah, 14, 14n9
Powell, General Colin, 94, 94n14
Proud Boys, 95, 129
Pseudo-christ, 13, 13n6
Purpose Driven Life, 5, 141
Putin, Vladimir, 19, 33, 69, 69n87, 89

QAnon, 120, 130n5, 132

Racism, racist, 22, 22n6, 30, 54n18, 64, 66, 69, 78, 83, 85, 92, 97, 116, 120, 136
Ramsey, Dave, 5
Raniere, Keith, 19
Ravitch, Richard, 63
Remini, Leah, 16, 16n15
Res, Barbara, 52, 52n8
Rodriguez, Carlos, 112
Roe v Wade, 9
Romney, Mitt, 92–93, 94n11
Roys, Julie, 111, 111n9

Scarborough, Joe, 62n49, 120
Scientology / Scientologists, 16–17, 31, 73
Scientology and The Aftermath, 16, 16n15
Scott, Sir Walter, 120n2
Searles, Cassandra, 44
Seduced, 17, 17n16
Settle For More, 23, 23–25n11–19
Sirleaf, Ellen Johnson, 72
Southern Baptist Convention, SBC, 26, 29–30, 134
Spiritual abuse, 29–30, 29n3
Stable Genius Act, 52
Stern, Howard, 37, 44, 44n2, 45

Thunberg, Greta, 26
Tillerson, Rex, 22, 60, 121
Tobias, Madeline, 18, 18n20
Trump, Donald, Quotes
    "You know, I'm automatically attracted to beautiful—I just start kissing. . .," xviin3, 44, 75
    "low I.Q. crazy," "bleeding badly from a face-lift," 8
    "I'm the only one," 12, 19, 64
    "I'm the only one who can fix our problems.," 13
    "I'm the only one that matters," 13
    "I alone can fix it," 13, 64
    "I am the chosen one," 13
    "Nobody has done more for Christianity. . .," 16, 78–79
    "Blood coming out of her . . . wherever," 22–23
    ". . . losers, dopes and babies," 22
    "bleeding badly from a face-lift," 23
    "You know why I do it? I do it to discredit you all. . .," 28
    "You know, he's killed reporters," 33
    "I hate them. I'd never kill them, but I do hate them. . .," 33
    "Believe me, if I become president, oh, do they have problems. . .," 33
    "And when you're a star they let you do it. You can do anything," 44, 75–76
    ". . .If I weren't happily married, and ya know, her father," 44
    "Wow! Just think—in a couple of years I'll be dating you," 46
    "Women. . . you have to treat them like s——," 47, 70, 107–8
    "You have the face of a dog," 47
    "You know, it doesn't really matter what they write. . .," 48
    " . . . and a very stable genius at that!," 52
    "I know words, I know the best words," 53
    "The final key to the way I promote is bravado. . .," 54
    "I could stand in the middle of Fifth Avenue and shoot somebody. . .," 54
    "The weak Republicans, they're pathetic Republicans. . .," 55
    "I play to people's fantasies. . . .," 61
    ". . .they don't look like Indians to me," 66

Trump, Donald, Quotes *(continued)*
  "The show is Trump, and it is sold out performances everywhere," 68
  "... Melania said this was OK," 76
  "... they are human scum!," 87
  "Big protest in DC on January 6th. Be there, will be wild!," 91n1, 93
  "Fight like hell!... Fight to the death," 96, 98
  "WE HAVE JUST BEGUN TO FIGHT!!!," 129, 129n1
  "'I Just Want to Find 11,780 Votes,'" 132n12
Trump, Fred Sr., 57–58, 63, 65–66, 131–33
Trump, Freddy, 56, 58, 69, 131–32
Trump, Ivana, 46, 52, 56, 61–62, 68
Trump, Mary, Ph.D, 49, 50, 58, 58n32, 66, 66n73, 69, 69n90, 71, 123n10, 129n2, 130–32, 132n10–11
Trump, Melania, 47, 56, 61n44, 76
Trump Organization, xii, 71, 71n98
Trump Plaza, 36, 108
Trump University, 24–25, 37, 67, 71
Trumpism, 10, 41–42, 82–83, 85, 101, 115
Tyson, Mike, 108
Tur, Katy, 22, 22n4, 32–34, 32n10–15, 33n16–18

Under the Banner of Heaven, 18, 18n19
Unholy: Why White Evangelicals Worship at the Altar of Donald Trump, 14, 14n9

Vanier, Jean, 31
Vow, The, 17, 17n16

Waco, 17, 17n16
Warren, Elizabeth, 26, 92
Warren, Rick, 5, 5n2, 112
Weinstein, Harvey, 31
White Nationalism, 30
White Supremacy, 19, 138
White, Paula, 13
Whittaker, Carlos, 112
Wild Wild Country, 17, 17n16
Willow Creek, 4, 31
Witmer, Gretchen, 26
Woodward, Bob, 121–23, 121n5, 122n6, 123n9

Yates, Sexton Jared, 34
Yousafzai, Malala, 72

Zacharias, Ravi, 31

Scripture Index

OT Scriptures

Gen
3:14–15   109n7

Lev
19:33   10n4

Deut
10:18–19   10n3

Jdgs
4:9   128n3
5:7   125
5:24–27   127n1

1 Kgs
14:16   82n3

2 Chron
7:14   138n2

Job
36:5   26n20

Ps
68:11   112n10
73:1–10   xviiin5
104:3   7n1

Prov
3:30–31   21
18:21   91, 92, 110
19:12   90
24:24   90
22:1–3   77n7
25:5   49
25:26   80
29:7   104n2

Hos
9:15   87n1

Mal
2:17   38n6

NT Scriptures

Matt

4:8–10	117n9
4:19	81n1
6:9–13	135n18
7:15–19	front
9:13	85n8
10:16	133n15, 134n16
12:34–37	87
15:18	43
18:6	107n2
23:2–7	16n14
24:4–5	12
24:24	13n6
25:35	10n5
25:40	40n1

Mark

7:20–23	83n4
8:15	xvin2, 81n2
10:42–45	115n3
13:22	13n6
14:6	106
14:10	xin1

Luke

2:52	117n7
4:1,14	117n8
4:18–19	85n9
6:45	47n20, 87n2
13:31	36n1
13:32	35, 36n2
21:8–9a	59n36

John

3:19–21	30, 30n7
3:20	29n5
8:7	106n1
8:44	121n4
12:4	xin1
12:7	xin2
20:17	128n2

Acts

3:19	137
3:19–20	136n1

Rom

2:11	31n8
13:1–2	29n2

1 Cor

1:7–9	99
10:14–22	97n20
10:20–21	98n22
15:33	27n21

2 Cor

2:14–16	40
3:17	138
7:1	43
11:12–15	134n17
11:3	xiii

Gal

1:6	83n5
5:19–21	15n11
6:7–8	87n1

Eph

5:11	32n9, 34n23

Phil

2:1–4	139v4
2:1–11	117n1
2:3–4	41
2:5	139v3
4:1	front

Col

3:5–8	78n9

1 Tim

6:2–5	37n5

2 Tim

1:7	72
3:1	15n12
3:5,13	37n4

Titus

3:10–11	15n10

Heb

4:13	34n24

Jas

1:13–15	131n8
3:13–16	119, 119n1
3:17–18	122n7
4:1–2	95n16
4:2	113

2 Pet

2:1–2	73n105
2:17–19	96n18, 129

1 John

3:8b	30n6
4:1	49
4:7	118n10

3 John

1:5–8	104n3
1:9–11	104n4

Jude

3–4	76n3
8	76n4, 79n11
12	76n5
16	77n6
16, 18–19	133n14
16–19	73n104
17–19	77n8

Rev

3:19	136

www.ingramcontent.com/pod-product-compliance
Lightning Source LLC
Chambersburg PA
CBHW030858170426
43193CB00009BA/661